ALONE
THE OBSERVER
*book of the Singlehanded
Transatlantic Race*

ALONE

THE OBSERVER

*book of the Singlehanded
Transatlantic Race*

by

DANIEL GILLES

with a Preface by

ERIC TABARLY

TRANSLATED BY
JOHN BUCHANAN-BROWN
AND EDITED BY FRANK PAGE,
YACHTING CORRESPONDENT OF
THE OBSERVER

ANGUS & ROBERTSON · PUBLISHERS

ANGUS & ROBERTSON · PUBLISHERS
London · Sydney · Melbourne · Singapore · Manila

First published in the United Kingdom by Angus and Robertson (UK) Ltd, 2 Fisher Street, London WC 1, in 1977.

Copyright © Editions du Neptune Nautisme et Editions du Pen-Duick 1976
Translation © Angus and Robertson 1977
ISBN 0 207 95758 4

Printed Litho in Great Britain by W & J Mackay Ltd, Chatham

CONTENTS

PREFACE by ERIC TABARLY

The Transatlantic Singlehanded Yacht Race is, in my opinion, the only race of its kind of any real significance. This arises from the fact that up to now it has been run with virtually no rules or regulations, leaving competitors completely free in their choice of boat, rig, and course. To compete you must, on the one hand, have a wide experience of the sea and of sailing so as to select your own craft, and on the other the qualities of seamanship, navigation and competitive spirit needed to take you over the finishing line in the shortest possible time.

In 1962 I heard about the second Transatlantic Singlehanded Race. My mind was soon made up: I wanted terribly to compete. As I saw it, it was the acme of ocean racing. I now had to solve a whole lot of problems: financial backing, choice of boat and training in single-handed sailing which was almost virgin territory for me. I was lucky enough to be ready in time for the start and then to win.

The Atlantic crossing did not change my mind about the race. I thought then, and I still think now, that this is indeed one of the finest ocean races.

Unfortunately financial considerations have restricted the field in this race and will continue to do so. In 1964 I was able to put the money together thanks to loans from friends, but this is something which is just no longer possible nowadays. The singlehanded yachtsman is now forced to find financial backing before he can enter the lists. Fortunately, the spectacular side of the contest gives a certain publicity value and this has led first in England and later in other countries to the appearance of the 'sponsor'. Thanks to him the race will survive.

This business and financial side has made some people say that the Singlehanded Race has become dull, because it has been reduced to a matter of money. You only need to glance at the results of previous races to see that statements like this simply are not true. The winning boats have never been the most expensive boats.

I should, however, be the last to deny the existence of financial problems, but once the money has been found it still has to be wisely spent in the design, choice and construction of the boat, and then the lone yachtsman who is to be her crew has to be a competent seaman. It is essential that rules should not be allowed to develop and restrictions be placed on the size of boat. If the race were restricted to small and medium craft, that is to boats of less than 65 feet, I think that then available financial resources would play a very large part and that there would even be the danger that they would falsify the results. If no competitor has to face problems of working his boat, as is the case with small craft, obviously in those circumstances equipment plays a very important role and means that fund-raising is the be-all. If we consider sailing as a sport and not just as an agreeable pastime, then the Singlehanded Race will have to be run with big boats.

My personal view of the ideal singlehanded race would be one fought out between mono- or multi-hull yachts of at least 72 feet. You would in any case have to race them in two different classes. Ideally all hulls would be standard, the choice of rig being left to each individual competitor. You would then be able to assess the sporting value of each contestant.

I suspect that one day such an event will be mounted.

In spite of everything, the Singlehanded Race has been and remains one of the finest contests on the high seas.

When we, at the publishers Éditions Pen Duick, considered commissioning a history of the race, we thought it only logical to seek a professional author who was also a professional seaman to write it.

Daniel Gilles, editor-in-chief of the magazine *Neptune-Nautisme* kindly accepted the task.

I got to know Daniel on board my *Pen Duick III*, when he sailed with us in 1967. He is a first-rate seaman, a prime crewman and good company into the bargain, as you need to be if you make up one of a crew. Of course he has been sailing since he was a boy and has been aboard many yachts, cruising, racing, and on many Atlantic crossings. In addition he took an active part in the working-up and trials of *Raph* in 1968. Finally, as a journalist on a specialist magazine, he has followed all the Singlehanded races in the closest detail.

I believe that he has succeeded in outlining in this book the problems raised by singlehanded sailing. He has described the races as they occurred, precisely and exactly yet at the same time without becoming too technical, so that anyone, even those who are unfamiliar with nautical matters, can understand what the Singlehanded Race is really like.

I hope this book will be widely read and that it will be widely appreciated how great a test of sporting skill takes place every four years on the Atlantic Ocean.

Editor's note: This was written before the Royal Western Yacht Club announced that the rules for the 1980 race would impose a maximum overall length limit of 56 feet (46 feet on the water-line) and a maximum fleet size of 110 yachts. The Club's reasons for making the new rules are, first, to avoid the possibility of the race presenting a hazard to other shipping in the English Channel soon after the start; second, to ensure that a greater proportion of the starters complete the course to America; and third, to promote a return to the original Hasler spirit of the race, in which the object was to overcome the Atlantic Ocean, rather than to conquer one's fellow competitors.

INTRODUCTION

Every four years the North Atlantic becomes the stage for a rather unusual sort of sea battle. Crossing the ocean under sail is a commonplace, nowadays; however, when the boat is manned by a solitary yachtsman, who has to perform all the duties of an entire crew, the crossing becomes very unusual indeed. The interest which this unusual race has aroused is perfectly reflected by the ever-growing number of competitors. The figures speak for themselves: in 1960, the year the race was first run, there were five; by the fifth contest in 1976 no less than 125 boats set sail for the New World. So, here we are dealing with something unique in the annals of ocean racing; its causes may be complex, but its success is basically due to two main factors — the simplicity of the rules and the efficiency of the organisers. For the latter, the sea and especially the race have few secrets. The personalities of the pioneers who shouldered the burden of the first race in 1960 inspire respect and are characteristic of those whose integrity and force of character make them outstanding. As far as the rules are concerned, nothing could be simpler: set out singlehanded from Plymouth aboard the boat of your choice and reach Newport, Rhode Island by whatever route you choose, and try to get there first. This is a simplicity designed to give yachtsmen their head and to encourage the production of new equipment, without the restriction which follows from complicated organisation and weight regulations or a handicap rule. Colonel 'Blondie' Hasler, the man who dreamt the whole enterprise up, intended to make this a contest of 'human performance'. He succeeded on all counts.

One of the difficulties at present is not so much spreading the news of the Singlehanded Race to potential new competitors (the race itself has shown that it has won its spurs), but far more to honour Hasler's conception of what it should be and keep it within reasonable bounds. As it is, the growing number of contestants begins to weigh heavily, not merely upon the organisers but upon those responsible for safety at sea. The fact that in every race the sheer size of the boats becomes ever greater is not calculated to make things any easier. The organisers of the event, the Royal Western Yacht Club, have started a snowball which grows bigger all the time — and they must not let it run away with them.

This book encompasses singlehanded sailing from its early days to the 1976 race and aims to give its readers a deeper understanding of one of the most fascinating contests of all time.

~~~~~~

CHAPTER ONE

Origins

Ocean racing is as old as sailing itself. Men of all ages have striven to set up their own records. The boats in the Singlehanded Race were not dreamed up in an instant, but are the heirs of a very ancient tradition established on all the world's seas. The part of it which relates to the North Atlantic has provided us with a chapter of outstanding interest.

Most yachtsmen are themselves the spiritual heirs of the old windjammer skippers who crossed the oceans to bring their freight safely home to port. Study of the history of seamanship under sail shows that whatever their rig and however many masts they carried, ships have always striven to sail as close as possible to the wind. Ever better refinements of hull forms and ever better-designed rigs have enabled them to do this. We shall see that today this is still one of the major problems of the east-west passage across the North Atlantic.

The first records of which seamen took account were those set up by the windjammers. With the wind behind them those towers of white canvas could log daily runs which were sensational in their day and can still surprise us now. The fastest run between London and Sydney, set up by the clipper *Patriarch,* 220 feet overall, still stood until very recently. This was the record and it was only beaten in March 1976 by two modern sailing ships. the English *Great Britain II* and the French *Kriter II. Patriarch* had taken sixty-nine days for the passage out to Australia and sixty-seven for the homeward run via the Cape. This was in 1870.

At that time commercial pressures drove owners and skippers to make fast passages. The first to dock could ask his own price. The fever which followed the first gold-strikes in California created a regular traffic between the eastern seaboard of the United States and San Francisco via Cape Horn. This avoided the long and dangerous journey by covered wagon across the Great Plains with their hostile Indians. In 1852 *Phoenician* docked in England with the first cargo of Australian gold.

From that time on, the Boston yards of Mackay were to become famous thanks to the orders from English ship-owners for clippers for their lines. Soon Donald Mackay was building the fastest sailing vessels in the world, most famous among them being the Australian wool-clipper *Lightning*. It seems that *Champion of the Seas,* from the same yard, recorded a run of 425 miles in twenty-four hours and that six of her contemporaries exceeded 400 miles in the same period. These records are all taken from Cyril Humer. However, although these ships really were very fast in wind conditions encountered below the fortieth parallel, these figures still seem exaggerated.

In his important work *A History of Seamanship,* Douglas Phillips-Birt makes a number of reservations about the validity of these records. In particular he quotes the authority of Captain Learmont:

He [Captain Learmont] first stresses the fact that by the time people became interested in accurate records of speed, the larger sailing ships had passed into history ... Captain Learmont takes a number of days' runs recorded in *Lloyds' Calendar,* and proceeds to demolish their claims. They all involve days' runs exceeding 400 miles, and the ships are the famous American clippers by Donald Mackay, which were built speculatively for the British market. Learmont points out that the conditions under which the ships were built and sold in-evitably encouraged excessive claims of speed. Secondly, the method of measuring speed through the water with a Yankee log and a sand-glass, used under the formidable conditions of wind and sea inevitable at times of fast sailing, was amenable to the grossest error, which Learmont estimates even as high as 5 knots ...

'Taking my long experience in sail into account [he says] I do not believe that any ship ever exceeded or even reached 400 miles in twenty-four hours under sail. I believe that the best days' run (noon to noon) ever to have been made under sail was that of the five-masted barque *Preussen,* when she made 370 miles under Captain Petersen in the South Pacific.'

Be this as it may, the first vessels to take the role of transoceanic racing craft were these large sailing ships. In 1860 the tea trade in-stigated the establishment of fresh records as these clippers raced to London with each new year's harvest. It soon became a sporting event for the crowds which turned out to watch for their arrival. In 1886, *Ariel* and *Taeping* finished their 13,000 mile voyage with a bare twenty minutes between them. The opening of the Suez Canal cut the time of the 'tea race' by half and ship-owners turned to Australia and the 'wool race'. This was the age of *Cutty Sark* and *Thermopylae*.

The early days of yachting were also deeply influenced by fishermen. Their craft were extremely seaworthy since they had to withstand the worst of the weather throughout the year, and experience gained from them went into the development of the yacht. One of the most famous examples of a Newfoundland banker converted for ocean racing was the *Bluenose*. Equal emphasis must be given to the pilot-cutter. Its magnificent lines and splendid rig made their own particular contribution, exemplified by the Le Havre pilot-cutter, *Jolie Brise,* winner of the first Fastnet Race in 1925. Thus, while the sailor went to sea to earn a living, there slowly emerged a new race of men who began to sail the oceans for the fun of it. These men were the pioneers of singlehanded sailing and some of them still remain famous. One of the first to make the singlehanded Atlantic crossing did so by force of circumstances. This was the famous Howard Blackburn, a working Banks fisherman. Like Joshua Slocum, one of the greatest seamen of all time, he was born in Nova Scotia, in 1858, and went to sea at the age of fifteen aboard ocean-going British and American sailing ships. In 1879 he settled in Gloucester, Mass, as a Banks fisherman. On 23 February 1883, having shipped aboard the schooner *Grace L. Fears* master John A. Griffin, his extraordinary story began.

As usual, he and another man had gone off cod-fishing in a dory, intending to return at nightfall to the mother-ship which remained hove to in the area during the day, when a violent south-westerly gale sprang up. The two fishermen were unconcerned since they were to windward of the schooner, but the wind soon shifted to the north-east and increased to storm force. Blackburn and Welch hauled in their lines, took to the oars and pulled in the general direction of the schooner, which soon vanished in a snow-squall. They anchored, hoping to find the schooner at dawn. At first light they saw her all right, but were unable to make sufficient headway against the gale to be rescued. The following night, in order to lighten the dory, the two fishermen were forced to bail and break off the ice which constantly formed on their craft.

Dawn broke and they were alone on the vast expanse of sea. While Welch at the oars held the dory steady, Blackburn fashioned a makeshift sea anchor to keep their head to the wind. While so doing Blackburn lost his mittens, a major disaster in such a low temperature, and he soon noticed that his hands were slowly losing their feeling and realised that this would stop him from rowing. Gathering the last remnants of his energy he forced his fingers round the grips of the oars and waited for his hands to freeze solid, so that he would then be able to row like his mate and take his share in saving both their lives. But Tom Welch died during the night and left Blackburn, utterly alone on the ocean, rowing for all his might. For five days he was without food and water, when he sighted land and managed to enter the mouth of a little river, the narrow estuary being flanked by high hills. He slept in an abandoned wooden hut and then continued upriver until at long last he reached a little fishing village, Little River. He lost all his fingers and the top joints of both thumbs. All his toes dropped off and he lost half his right foot as well.

Despite all this, a few months later he shipped aboard a schooner bound for San Francisco round the Horn, proving that this amazing character's sailing days were by no means over. Later on he had a 30 foot boat built to sail from Gloucester, Mass to Gloucester, England. Setting out in June 1899, he made the passage after sixty-one days at sea.

On his return to the United States, Blackburn, on 1 January 1901, issued, through the press, a challenge to any American singlehanded sailor to race against him on the Gloucester-Lisbon run, and to back it deposited his stake with the secretary of the East Gloucester Yacht Club. His *Great Republic* was the sole contender on 9 June 1901. After a thirty-nine-day crossing, he moored in the port of Lisbon on 18 July! Following this, Blackburn had adventures on the Great Lakes, descended the Mississippi and was shipwrecked on the Florida coast.

His last exploit was to set off across the North Atlantic in a sailing dory in an effort to beat the record set up by Alfred Johnson, who had crossed in a cutter-rigged dory with a square foresail in 1876. Three times Blackburn turned turtle and each time, strange as this may sound, he succeeded in righting the dory, but he had to give up and return for home. Blackburn died when he was over seventy, having made voyages which, although they are almost beyond belief, showed what could be done with small boats, sailed, admittedly, by someone outside the common run of men.

Howard Blackburn is, in a way, the first of the North Atlantic racing yachtsmen. However, when discussing singlehanded sailing, mention must be made of the first singlehanded circumnavigation of the world, made by Joshua Slocum aboard his 37-foot *Spray*. He set sail from Boston on 24 April 1895, and completed the round-trip of 46,000 miles on 27 June 1898, having crossed the Atlantic to Gibraltar, headed for South America, rounded Cape Horn through the Straits of Lemaire, crossed the Pacific, coasted the eastern seaboard of Australia, clearing the northern tip through the Torres Straits, having gone on across the Indian Ocean, round the Cape of Good Hope, back up the Atlantic again, touching the West Indies before returning to Boston. In those days yachtsmen were few on the water and wherever he went Slocum received a delightful welcome, although he did have to repel attacks by savages in the estuaries of Patagonia.

Joshua Slocum is, however, known not merely as the first lone circumnavigator, but as one of the greatest, and his log introduces the reader to a rare and engaging character who pointed the way for his many successors, among them Bernard Moitessier who christened his boat *Joshua* in memory of the man he worshipped.

16

There has never been any reservation about the enthralling voyage of *Spray* across all the oceans of the world. The stories, and there are plenty of them in that great seaman's book, make us realise that the boat which he had built was incredibly seaworthy — particularly so for her day. *Spray's* great stability was due to the breadth of her beam and to the balance of her sail plan which Slocum had adjusted in South America to make her more easy to handle. The fact that the voyage, all 46,000 miles of it, was completed without the use of self-steering gear, shows how well conceived was this amazing little yacht. The account which Slocum left is extraordinarily rich and evocative. There is great humour in the portraits of the people he met, his descriptions of the magnificent scenery perfectly recreate his voyage in our mind's eye, and the picture of his boat, that faithful travelling companion, is lovingly painted. At the end of his wonderful voyage, Slocum wrote in *Sailing Around the World:*

I had profited in many ways by the voyage . . . I was at least ten years younger than the day I felled the first tree for the construction of the *Spray.*
My ship was also in better condition than when she sailed from Boston on her long voyage. She was still as sound as a nut, and as tight as the best ship afloat. She did not leak a drop — not one drop! The pump, which had been little used before reaching Australia, had not been rigged since that at all . . .
If the *Spray* discovered no continents on her voyage, it may be there were no more continents to be discovered. She did not seek new worlds, or to sail to pow-wow about the dangers of the seas. The sea has been much maligned. To find one's way to lands already discovered is a good thing, and the *Spray* made the discovery that even the worst sea is not so terrible to a well-appointed ship . . .
To succeed, however, in anything at all, one should go understandingly about his work and be prepared for every emergency.

The first east-west crossing was by Alain Gerbault in his *Firecrest,* a 39-foot cutter, taking one hundred and one days for the voyage from Gibraltar to New York in 1923. This was a 'first' of some importance, since the prevailing winds in the North Atlantic are westerlies. It is true that twenty-eight years earlier, Slocum had crossed the Atlantic in this direction, but he had done so at a much lower latitude in order to take advantage of the prevailing trade winds there. Not until 1948 did a yacht repeat Alain Gerbault's feat. The press gave Gerbault's crossing a great deal of coverage and the Frenchman gained wide popularity, but it annoyed many people to see all this fuss about a crossing accompanied by so many mishaps of split sails and clumsy handling. When Gerbault made the Atlantic crossing he was little better than a novice yachtsman, and those who earned their living under sail (and there were still plenty of them in those days), or who simply sailed for pleasure but knew and respected the sea, were shocked by the way in which Gerbault undertook it. Later on, Gerbault had plenty of time to learn, since he was to sail singlehanded virtually every ocean around the world!

Captain Graham was the first to link Ireland and Newfoundland by the northern sea route, taking twenty-four days aboard his 30-foot cutter, *Emmanuel,* in 1934. Ann Davidson was the first woman to make the crossing from Plymouth to New York in her sloop, *Felicity Ann.* The year was 1952.

The start of transatlantic yacht racing really goes back to 1866. We now leave the isolated exploits of lone sailors, for racing with a full crew. This is the year of the race between three schooners, *Vesta* (105 feet), *Fleetwing* and *Henrietta,* from the Sandy Hook Light Vessel to England. After eight days at sea, a breaking wave washed eight men from the decks of *Fleetwing.* Two of them managed to struggle back on board again, but some hours later the schooner got under way again without having been able to rescue the others. *Vesta* was the first to sight the Bishop Rock Lighthouse on Christmas night. *Henrietta* was fifty minutes behind, but managed to regain the lead in the last 200 miles to Cowes on the Isle of Wight. Her time of thirteen days, twenty-one hours, and forty-five minutes is a fantastic average over a distance of nearly 3000 miles. *Fleetwing* reached Cowes eight hours behind the victor and forty minutes ahead of *Vesta.*

There were few major races after that 'first'. The 120-foot schooner *Dauntless* lost two of them, one to *Cambria* (challenger for the famous America's Cup in 1870), the course being from Daunt Head in Ireland to Sandy Hook; the other to the schooner *Coronet* in 1887, the course being from Sandy Hook to Cork in Ireland. From 1851, the year in which the schooner *America* crossed to Europe, until 1905, there were forty-five Atlantic crossings, thirty-five of them being from west to east. These schooners were all handled by large, well-trained crews of professional seamen, but it is interesting and relevant to record their feats even if most of their passages were west-east, exactly the opposite to the course laid down by Colonel Hasler sixty-odd years later.

Eleven yachts took part in the 1905 race, varying in size from the 105-foot *Fleur de Lys,* the smallest boat, to the largest, the 240-foot *Valhalla,* a square-rigged three master. Many of the owners were on board, which was unusual for the period, and some even carried passengers in addition to the master and the professional crew. The winner was the schooner, *Atlantic,* in a record time which has never yet been beaten — twelve days, four hours, and one minute on a course from Sandy Hook to Lizard Point, a distance of 3014 miles. This splendid three-masted schooner was 180 feet overall, no great size when compared with some of her competitors, but she had been wonderfully designed by William Gardner. Let it also be said that her skipper was Charlie Barr, famed for his victories in the America's Cup, and he pushed the aptly christened *Atlantic* to her very limits. So much so, that legend has it that one night he continued to carry so much sail in a squall that the owner, Wilson Marshall, and the passengers fell to the deck on their knees and prayed! For the next forty years *Atlantic* was to make other crossings and she will always be admired as one of the most efficient sailing machines of all time. There have also been plenty of attempts to break her fabulous record, which stands at an average speed of 10.4 knots. During World War II she was used as a sail training ship by cadets of the US Coastguard Service and tragically ended her days as a floating tea-shop, eventually foundering in the shallows off a New Jersey resort.

It was not until 1928 that the next transatlantic race took place and it was the last to be run with professional crews. Two classes based on the water-line length were to sail concurrently. The winner of the larger was *Elena,* designed by the famous American naval architect, Herreshoff, and owned by William Bell, with John Barr, nephew of the famous Charlie, as skipper. Second was none other than *Atlantic,* carrying far less canvas than in the year of her record!

Victory in the class for boats of 33 to 52 feet water-line length went to *Nina,* designed by another famous American naval architect, Burgess, with Paul Hammond as skipper, by a narrow margin over *Pinta* and *Mohawk.*

Later, yacht design developed enormously. Those splendid schooners like *Atlantic* vanished and professional crews gave way to amateurs, and the 1931 race marked the beginning of a new era in ocean racing. Oddly enough the race that year was in exactly the opposite direction to the Singlehanded Race — from Newport, Rhode Island, to Plymouth, England. It was the first time that so many different rigs had assembled for the same race and they foreshadowed the shapes of the boats which sail our waters today. This was the first appearance of the American naval architect, Olin Stephens, with his famous yawl, *Dorade,* which won the race in seventeen days, setting course along the Great Circle route to take advantage of the stronger wind conditions to be found there. We shall see that this was the route taken by the five victors in the Singlehanded Race, although in their case in the opposite direction.

In 1935 there was another victory for a boat designed by Stephens — the yawl *Stormy Weather* — in the race from Newport to Bergen in Norway. Then ocean races were regularly organised from Bermuda to England or Germany, or from Havana to a Spanish port, or again from the USA to Marstrand in Sweden. The last named was won by *Carina,* a name well-known in American yacht-racing circles, designed by Philip Rodes, and she covered the 3450 miles in twenty days, nine hours, and seventeen minutes. She was one of the first centreboard yachts and her beam gave her plenty of space below decks. *Carina* reappeared in the 1957 Newport to Santander race.

Since that time these races have become regular events, drawing together each year some of the finest craft afloat. They serve as the connecting link between the equally prestigious regattas which take place on either side of the ocean. Europe and America have unified their system of handicapping and more and more yachts will be voyaging between the two continents, to the added delight of those gluttons for mileage, the ocean racers.

Thus those who enter for the Singlehanded Race are the heirs of a long tradition of ocean racing as well as of the particular experience gained by those who have ploughed the seas alone for the pleasure of achieving epic voyages. One must take all this into account if one is properly to understand the idea which Colonel 'Blondie' Hasler had in 1960, after having recorded some remarkable racing successes in 1946 with his 30 square metre, *Tre-Sang.*

CHAPTER TWO

~~~~~~

Hasler's Idea

'Blondie' Hasler was the first person to think of a singlehanded race across the Atlantic. He even put up the scheme to the Slocum Society of New York in 1956. However, the Americans hesitated at that time because of the risks inherent in such an undertaking.

The one thing that could be said about Hasler's ideas were that they were original, for he was a man with a talent for the unorthodox. In 1941, as a captain in the Royal Marines, he successfully put forward the ground-plan of a raid designed to blow up shipping in the port of Bordeaux, then under German occupation. Ten men with collapsible canoes were released from a submarine in the Gironde estuary, managed to plant their charges on the hulls of six merchant ships and to sink them. Only Hasler and one other Marine were to return from the operation. This is a strong enough indication of the character of the man and explains his liking for doing the thing which is out of the ordinary and requires guts. When Hasler retired from the Marines with the rank of Colonel, he did not lose touch with the sea and continued to sail and to race. In 1952 he had a boat of his own built which was to become world famous, for *Jester* was to be on every Singlehanded Race from 1960 onwards.

The idea continued to buzz around his brain. After discussions with various English clubs, the Royal Western Yacht Club agreed to organise the race with the strong support of the American Slocum Society.

Although some people held back, the enterprise still went ahead, thanks to a tiny group of men like Chichester, then a mere beginner and quite unknown in yachting circles, who was to become the famous Sir Francis, one of the finest seamen of the twentieth century. Christopher Brasher, Sports Editor of *The Observer,* was to be no stranger to the story of the Singlehanded Race, since he was to become its passionate advocate, deeply involved in the planning, suggesting acceptable alterations to the programme in 1959 and last but not least securing the backing of his paper. From this point on all the requisite elements were to hand for the official launching of the race. The Royal Western Yacht

Club was there to handle technical matters and *The Observer* to underwrite the idea and put it over to the general public. Some English sports columnists no more than remarked on the courage of *The Observer*, while in Parliament there was a Question condemning the race on the grounds that it would be impossible to control.

In fact as far as the top brass among English yachtsmen were concerned the whole concept of the race was sheer madness—it was something entirely new to them — they were used to racing with a full crew. What would be the public reaction if anything went wrong? During a meeting at which the feasibility of the entire project was still under discussion, Chichester got up to announce that if nobody was prepared to organise the race, he and 'Blondie' Hasler were ready to tackle the Atlantic for a side-bet of half-a-crown. The Americans were vastly taken up by the challenge, and as they did not know what half-a-crown was they changed the bet to five shillings.

What in any case was this 'idea' which was so often discussed in the bars of yacht clubs along the south coast of England? It was quite simple and straightforward, which is what made it both vastly interesting and at the same time deeply disturbing. Hasler prescribed the unpalatable notion of 'one man, one boat, and the Atlantic Ocean'. This meant that he was going against all the rules when he said that his intention was for the race to be run on elapsed time and that the only limit would be set by the yachtsman himself in his choice of boat. Quite apart from the fact that this extraordinary character sought to inaugurate an event designed to enhance individual skill and endurance, he was also convinced — rightly as it turned out — that this was the best way of stimulating technical progress.

This, then, was the underlying motive of the first Singlehanded Race: the contestant would be the only person on board and hence he alone would have to perform all the functions of a seaman. This meant that he would have to make his boat ready down to the tiniest detail, thus forcing him to innovate and work out the best methods of proper and speedy handling of boat and sails. The first fruit of this research was the self-steering gear which keeps a boat under sail on course without anyone at the tiller. This invention, so useful to yachtsmen as a whole and about which I shall have more to say later, was one of Hasler's brainwaves. Well before the first Singlehanded Race, he had for his own amusement perfected the self-steering gear which bears his name and which is carried by so many cruising yachts today. Nor should the Colonel's experiments with rig be overlooked either. *Jester* had originally been provided with a Lungström rig, but actually raced with a Chinese lugsail, a sail-plan better suited to the singlehanded yachtsman and one which the Chinese had perfected over thousands of years. The lugsail is a fully battened square sail which can be raised or lowered by a series of control lines rather like a venetian blind. It is not as efficient as a conventional fore-and-aft rig, but it can be reefed and unreefed very quickly from the yacht's cockpit. It therefore eliminates the labours and dangers of a singlehander changing sails or reefing on a bucking deck during heavy weather. Joshua Slocum, one of the greatest seamen of all time, and the first person to complete the circumnavigation of the world singlehanded under sail in 1898, had himself used this rig in 1890, when he took his family from Buenos Aires to New England on a very swift passage, the best day's run being 150 miles. In his search for the greatest speed compatible with solo handling, Hasler revived the rig as most suitable for the style of sailing which he had in mind.

These two examples define exactly the spirit of the first singlehanded races. Sheer physical strength plays a very important role when one is sailing, but it is not the complete answer. Technical innovation gains an added value for singlehanded sailors. Another factor which helps to develop races of this sort is the difficulty of getting together a crew which is both professionally competent and at the same time a harmonious unit. This is a problem which is seldom solved completely satisfactorily. This simple fact explains why at this very moment so many lone sailors plough the seas in complete freedom, accountable to none but themselves — it is a purely relative freedom, of course, since sooner or later they will learn how rigorous a discipline the sea demands of them.

The best route for the race was soon determined. At first glance it was obvious that it would have to be held during the summer in the North Atlantic. Apart from the symbolic value of linking the Old World with the New, there was the fact that weather conditions would then be ideally suited to a contest of this kind. The race starts from England, which is at the receiving end of the prevailing Atlantic winds and currents, so the competitors have to sail into the teeth of them. This makes conditions all the harder and the race all the more enthralling. The immediate problem is to reconcile the various elements involved: whether to take the shortest route — about 3000 miles — which means beating to windward most of the way and risking ice and fog near the American seaboard; whether to head south to sunshine and reaching winds, which means lengthening the distance to be sailed to about 3500 miles; or whether to head north, looking for possible following easterlies, perhaps dodging the great Atlantic rollers, yet despite all this running the risk of sailing another 250 miles. This is a fascinating exercise in which the characteristics of the boat are an all-important factor. Fast sailing close-hauled demands a particular sail-plan and a distinct type of boat. Sailing with the wind implies that the boat should be light enough to gain the speed to have any chance of making headway against heavier, tougher boats with a shorter daily run, but less distance to cover

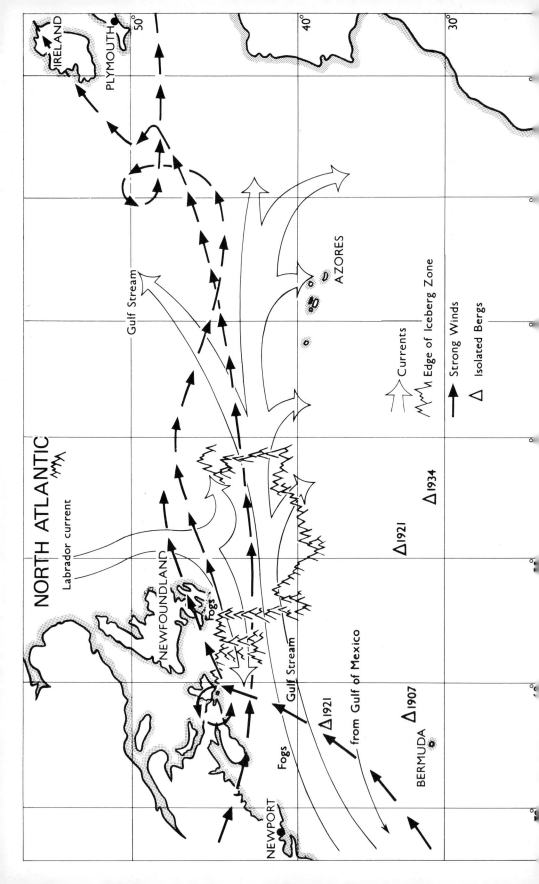

NORTH ATLANTIC

Labrador current

Gulf Stream

NEWFOUNDLAND

Fogs

IRELAND

PLYMOUTH

50°

40°

30°

AZORES

BERMUDA

NEWPORT

Gulf Stream

Fogs

from Gulf of Mexico

△1921

△1907

△1921

△1934

Currents

Edge of Iceberg Zone

Strong Winds

△ Isolated Bergs

overall. This makes a most intriguing sum to solve, particularly so when human and boat factors are taken into account as well.

The Royal Western Yacht Club could not be better situated geographically to run a westbound race. Located in Plymouth on the south-west coast, it satisfies the first essential, that is to allow the competitors to clear the Channel right from the start. The shore is always the seaman's foe, never more so than to the singlehanded sailor who cannot guarantee a twenty-four-hour watch and needs to be on the open sea as soon as possible. Then, too, the short stretch of the Channel to be covered holds another danger — that of being run down, especially by a freighter on a fixed course, or by a trawler. This is what makes the first few days of the race such a strain on the nerves, and history shows that it is essential to keep a careful watch. The Royal Western Yacht Club was the perfect choice, too, as race organiser since it is an old established club, with a lot of experience and traditions behind it. Furthermore it was familiar to yachtsmen since it had been responsible since 1925 for playing host to the competitors in that most celebrated of ocean racing events, the Fastnet Race.

The finishing line for the first Singlehanded Race was New York. From 1964 onwards this was replaced by Newport, Rhode Island, one of the busiest yachting centres of the United States. The wide Narragansett bay, spanned by an enormous bridge, is a favourite place for sailing enthusiasts. The celebrated races for the America's Cup are held offshore which no challenger has yet been able to snatch from American hands. Newport is also the starting point for the famous Bermuda Race, which has been regularly run since 1905. The cold Labrador Current, sweeping south along the coast of Newfoundland to meet the warm land-mass causes the fogs which so often blanket the finishing line of the Singlehanded Race. It often makes the last few miles run extremely difficult and exceedingly tricky to plot position accurately.

Before 1960 there had only been one east-west race against the prevailing winds. This took place in 1870 between two large schooners, each with a sizable crew. The vessels concerned were *Dauntless* and *Cambria*. The former, nearly 136 feet in length and with a crew of thirty-nine, lost the race because she was forced to search, and search in vain, for two members of the crew who had been swept overboard when working for'ard. Thus the winner was the superb and majestic schooner *Cambria,* with a bare hour and thirty-seven minutes in hand. Remembering that the distance to be covered was very nearly 3000 miles the difference between the two was minuscule.

To return to the first Singlehanded Race, which was due to start from Plymouth on 11 June 1960 and finish in New York. There was no set route, no limit on the competing yachts, and no specification as to rig or

25

hull. The boat had to be driven by the wind, that was all, and if there was an engine aboard its use was restricted to charging batteries for lighting, radio and navigational instruments. Self-steering gear was permitted, but it could not be mechanically powered by the engine. Finally no outside assistance was allowed during the course of the race and, of course, only one person was to be on each boat. These, roughly, were the basic rules which were to govern the first two races. In 1968 they were made more elaborate in view of the growing success of the event and the increasing numbers of competitors.

Although I have already said that the simplicity of the rules was half the attraction of the race for its competitors, I am forced to admit, with the advantage of hindsight, that it would soon set very serious problems. Without wishing at this stage to go into the 1968 and 1976 races, I must now touch upon one or two technical aspects if the spirit in which the race is sailed is to be clear.

The original idea of placing no limit upon size and of using no system of handicapping, was immensely attractive for the first race ever. However, the theorem that states that the speed of a boat is proportionate to the square root of her water-line length, forces competitors to enter boats of ever-increasing size, if they are to stand any chance of winning. The longer a boat, the faster it will travel. And in the first two races, length was the key to success. In 1960, Chichester's 39-foot yawl was 14 foot longer than any of his rivals' boats. Four years later Eric Tabarly won in *Pen Duick II* which measured 33 feet on the water-line, a size at the time considered impossible for a singlehanded sailor to handle. These two set the standards for the race and gave it the prestige which it now enjoys. It never entered the heads of Hasler or Chichester, when they launched the event in 1960, that sixteen years later a 236-foot boat would be specially prepared for it. They could not imagine that a lone sailor could handle a boat of this size. Yet *Club Méditerranée* was sailed singlehanded from Plymouth to Newport in 1976 even if it did not win the race.

Tabarly's victory in 1964 brought a new emphasis on length into the game which tended to overshadow the ground-rules. It did not in any way deform Hasler's brainchild, but made it develop in a slightly different direction. After all, technical improvement was one of the guiding principles at the outset, and so it remains; it has even surpassed all reasonable expectations. All the same, the race should not produce sailing monsters, owing their victory solely to the money behind them and not sportsmanship. By keeping to the same essentials it should still be possible to continue to encourage research, at the same time setting limitations upon water-line length in order to operate a control upon experimentation. A first approach would be a system of classification by size, and this, in fact, was put into operation in 1976, and now the Royal

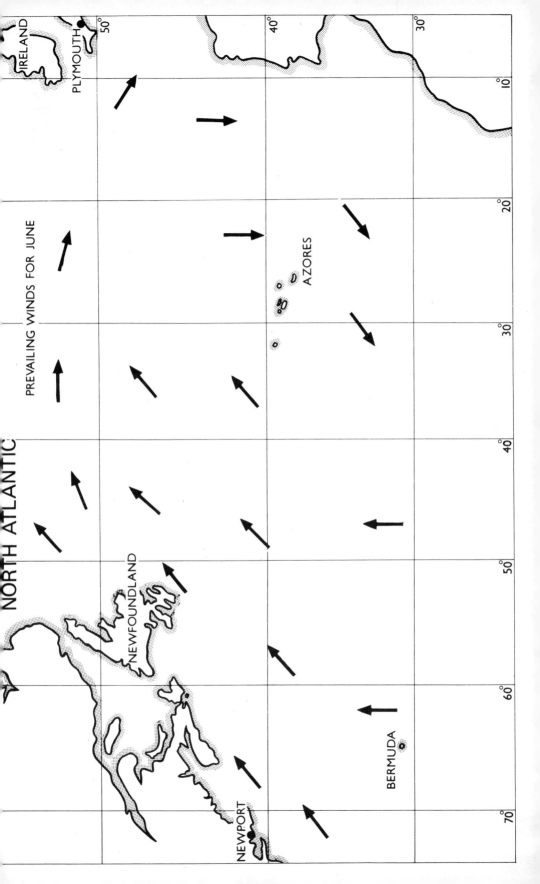

Western proposes an overall size limit of 56 feet (46 feet water-line) for the 1980 race. *Pen-Duick II* seemed a big boat in 1964. It is a good thing that she was tuned to racing pitch, because she provided the proof that a well-trained man could handle a boat of this size on his own. Actually, although the length of the *Pen-Duick II* is important, what is still more important is the basic concept, for she was specially designed for the race, that is to say with a very light displacement for the time when she was built — and that also had its influence on the result.

Length means speed in sailing vessels. It also influences weight, and this in turn determines the cost of construction. The heavier the boat, the more she will cost, so that to increase the length boils down to a matter of finance. All the same there seems to be no reason why, beyond a certain length, a relatively smaller craft designed to other principles of speed should not sooner or later defeat the big boats. Multi-hulls have in a way already proved the case. Boats like Mike Boldi's *The Third Turtle* (1976) and Tom Follett's (1968) *Cheers,* represent a line of research far more interesting than the giant mono-hull. Just as Tabarly was the man who managed to win in 1964 by building a boat ideally suited for that race, he is still a pioneer in his work on a new family of ultra-light craft, mounted on hydrofoils, and he should have had one ready for the start of the 1976 race if time had not been too short to work it up. Here is an idea (with all the technical innovations it contains for singlehanded ocean racing), which should delight the man who invented the race.

The 1976 race has contributed its tithe of experience and the Committee has now promulgated a new set of rules. These are clearly designed to curb the ever-increasing size of competing yachts, which not only confounded the founders' original intentions, but were a positive safety hazard. The new rules mean that we have been watching yet another turning-point in the history of the Singlehanded Race — the passing of the dinosaurs. The arrival of the multi-hulls (of which more later) and the elimination of the giants shows that a race as enthralling as the Singlehanded always has a fresh surprise in store and is very far from becoming just another event on the yachting calendar.

CHAPTER THREE

1960: The Inaugural Race

On 11 June 1960, the early morning mist was just lifting from the city of Plymouth. The harbour was still following the easy rhythm of early summer and there was nothing to show that the four entries for the first singlehanded transatlantic race were making last-minute preparations for getting under way on a voyage which would make its mark in the annals of sail.

The competitors had gathered in Millbay Dock, where a dock-gate protected them from the rise and fall of the tide. It was not a particularly cheerful place for yachts: the murky waters were normally occupied by small cargo boats and coasters, and cranes stood black and gloomy against the skyline.

The race had caused scarcely a ripple of interest amongst the world's press. Very few journalists had even heard about it, but some of them did turn up out of curiosity. Though the race was hardly front-page news in England a fair number of ocean racing enthusiasts had foregathered in Plymouth, drawn by the forceful personality of Colonel Hasler, whose Bordeaux Raid was still remembered; and by Chichester, whose feats as a pilot had made him well-known to the public 20 years before. In any case there were plenty of friends on hand, as Chichester recounts in *The Lonely Sea and the Sky*.

> On the night before the race, Sheila and I decided to have a quiet dinner together with Giles at Pedro's. Lindley Abbott of *The Observer* asked me if he and his wife could join us, and before we had finished it was a dinner party of seventy people. I always intend to start an ocean race with a clear head, after no drink taken. Perhaps one day I shall succeed, but that night I remember walking up to the Hoe after the party with Mike Richey, secretary of the Institute of Navigation, and a very experienced ocean racer. Sheila asserts that at 1 o'clock in the morning we were trying to get a star fix from a street lamp.

On the morning of the start, the competitors left the dock-basin on the flood tide.

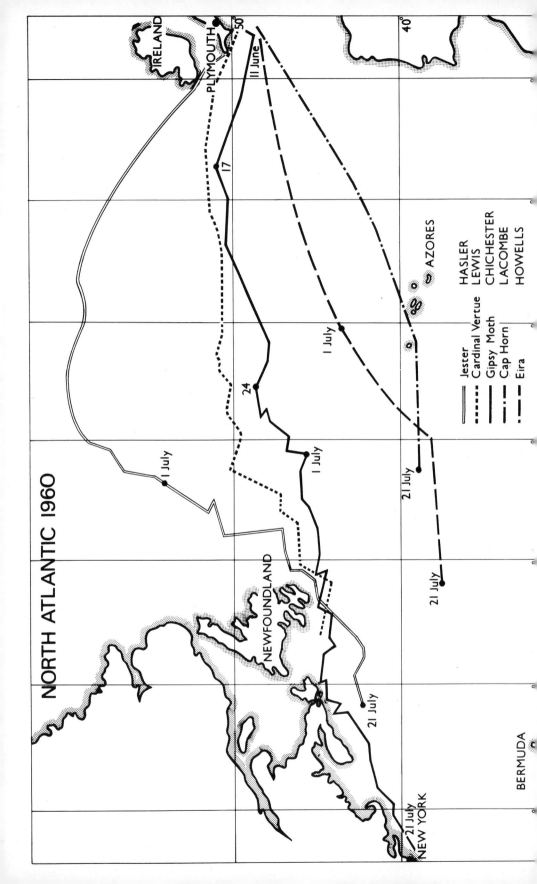

NORTH ATLANTIC 1960

IRELAND

PLYMOUTH

50

40

11 June

17

24

AZORES

1 July

1 July

1 July

1 July

21 July

21 July

21 July

NEWFOUNDLAND

21 July

21 July
NEW YORK

BERMUDA

Jester	HASLER
Cardinal Vertue	LEWIS
Gipsy Moth	CHICHESTER
Cap Horn	LACOMBE
Eira	HOWELLS

Francis Chichester's boat, *Gipsy Moth III,* was a yawl 39 feet long, with a displacement of 13 tons, which was rather heavy for its size. Built in wood on traditional lines, with a deep keel and lofty rigging, her foresails were of an impressive area, particularly when they were set on their own. Her skipper had bought her in 1954 and had entered this inaugural race at the age of fifty-eight, and he was a man with the diabolical habit of succeeding in whatever venture he undertook — as is only too clear from a study of his long-distance flights which broke new ground in exactly the same way as his feats of seamanship.

Colonel Hasler was there on board the popular *Jester,* which was to make her mark in all the Singlehanded Races. *Jester* remains a sort of standard bearer, having taken part in each of the five races to date. A Folkboat, 25 feet in length, *Jester* was strangely rigged, with a fully battened Chinese lugsail on an unstayed mast. Unlike her sister ships, she was completely decked over with a small circular hatch on the cabin roof, from which it was possible to work the boat and keep lookout. It is amusing to remember Hasler saying just before the start that a radio set was useless and that a small boat could well do without weather forecasts, since you don't need to know what the weather is going to be to handle a boat. *Jester's* sail area, he remarked, was small anyway and could be made still smaller very rapidly. On previous crossings he had used a barometer, but it had become something of a nuisance by lowering his morale. Lack of a radio receiver made it vital that his chronometer should be absolutely accurate when he used his sextant. To avoid any error he was taking with him four chronometers which he had been scrupulously regulating for the past month so that they would provide a check the one on the others. He also had his cassette-player and plenty of tapes of jazz to listen to occasionally, plus his ukelele and a pile of *New Yorker* magazines which he had not had time to read at home before the race.

Val Howells, too, had entered a Folkboat christened *Eira,* but it retained the conventional sloop rig. Howells himself was thirty-six at the time of the inaugural race and was farming in Pembrokeshire after many years in the Merchant Navy.

David Lewis had been brought up in New Zealand before returning to England where he practised as a doctor. He was then forty-three and had entered *Cardinal Vertue,* a 25-foot yacht belonging, as its name would suggest, to the Vertue-class designed by the English naval architect Laurent Giles in 1936. He had qualified for the race by making a round-trip to Norway and back singlehanded, He lost his mast almost at the start of the race and was forced back to Plymouth for repairs before setting off once more in pursuit of his rivals.

The only Frenchman to enter did not reach port in England until the eve of the race with a long list of adjustments to be made to his boat. He

1. Colonel 'Blondie' Hasler, inventor of and moving spirit behind the Singlehanded Race.

2. *Tre-Sang* the 30 sq. m. Skerry Cruiser built in 1934. First example of the light displacement ocean racer, Hasler took her to victory in the RORC Class III in 1946.

3. *Gipsy Moth II,* the boat on which Sir Francis Chichester won his sailing spurs.

4. The famous Gipsy Moth seaplane used by Chichester for so many of his famous flights, including the solo crossing of the Tasman Sea.

5. Only five competitors entered for the first race. The start from Plymouth with *Cardinal Vertue* in the foreground.

6. *Cap Horn,* the smallest boat to be entered, with her skipper, Jean Lacombe (7).

8. The enclosed deck of *Jester,* Hasler's junk-rigged Folkboat.

9. Valentine Howells aboard *Eira.*

10. Sir Francis Chichester, outright winner of the first race, and his *Gipsy Moth III* (11).

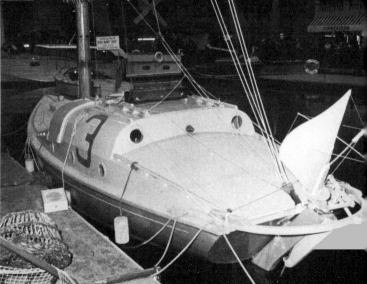

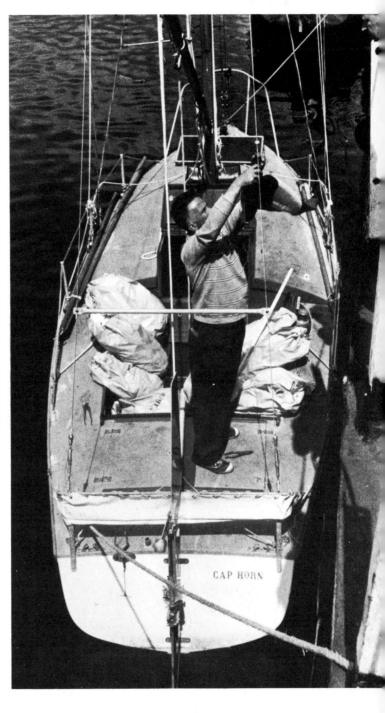

GIPSY MOTH

1960—Francis Chichester—*Gipsy Moth III*—40 days 12 hrs 30 mins

Length: 39 feet (mono-hull)
Traditional wooden-built hull
Sloop-rigged with 7/8ths jib
Architect: Robert Clark
Built in Ireland

was to start five days late. This was Jean Lacombe with *Cap Horn*. The boat had been held up in the yard while modifications were carried out below-decks and self-steering gear, designed by the French naval architect Jean-Jacques Herbulot, was fitted. It was a 21-foot boat with a centreboard, built for coastal cruising rather than for ocean racing. Lacombe, who was forty-four, had already crossed the Atlantic on *Hippocampe,* a boat he had built himself. He worked as a journalist and news-photographer in New York and had snatched the opportunity of entering the race by taking delivery of *Cap Horn* from the yard and sailing her over to New York for her new owner.

The five men came from very different backgrounds but they had one thing in common, they looked on this Atlantic crossing as a challenge. In that first race there were no constants. It was assumed that the bigger the boat the better the chances of winning, but there were so many unknown factors, not least of them being the choice of route. That year all the competitors except Lacombe owned the boats they were racing in, and nobody had thought of building a yacht especially for the race. Each hoped to come in first, but all set off also intending to enjoy their common adventure and to discover the limits of their own endurance. There was a single objective but five different ways of achieving it.

From the spectator's point of view the start itself was not dramatic. But you need to have experienced an ocean race start to know what it feels like. Some people may think you have all the time in the world when starting an event which is going to last forty or fifty days. Experienced racers, however, know that this is the vital moment, even in a long-distance race. Chichester thoroughly appreciated this point: he reached the start under his No 1 genoa headsail which he had hoisted a few seconds before the gun went off. The start was a line from the umpire's boat to the Melampus Buoy, which had to be passed to starboard a few hundred yards from Drake's Island within Plymouth Sound. The next mark, and the only one, was the Ambrose Light Vessel, anchored outside the port of New York. The first week was not an easy time, as Francis Chichester recounts:

> For the first three days the weather was rough with gales. Heavy seas burst on the deck, and I reckoned that it took thirty seconds after a sea had broken on deck before the water finished running out of the lee scuppers. I had considered *Gipsy Moth* a dry boat apart from one or two minor leaks, and I had pumped no water out of her during the three months she had been afloat. After the first three days, however, all the cabin walls were streaked as if they had been in a slanting shower of rain. . . .
>
> My chest was hurting me on one side where I had been thrown across the yacht when a door burst open forward; on the other side it had been stabbed by a sharp corner when the cabin hatch, which I was leaning against, suddenly slipped forward a foot; a patch of skin over my ribs had been caught in a doorway when the door slammed on it, and I had cut my scalp on the roof of the cabin. Then my seasickness ended, and it was not long before I was recording that I would not change places with anybody in the world.
>
> I got steadily more skilful in handling the yacht. . . .

Apart from the ceaseless struggle to handle his boat and to establish a daily routine aboard her, the most vital problem for the lone sailor is that of keeping a lookout. While sailing through busy waters, he cannot risk sleeping for any length of time for fear of colliding with another vessel. So long as he is anywhere near land he must keep on watch constantly because, although his self-steering gear will maintain the boat's angle to the wind, if the wind changes the boat is thrown completely off course. The danger is all the more increased if the lone sailor has to make a prolonged physical effort, such as in variable wind conditions when he must constantly change and trim the sails for maximum speed,

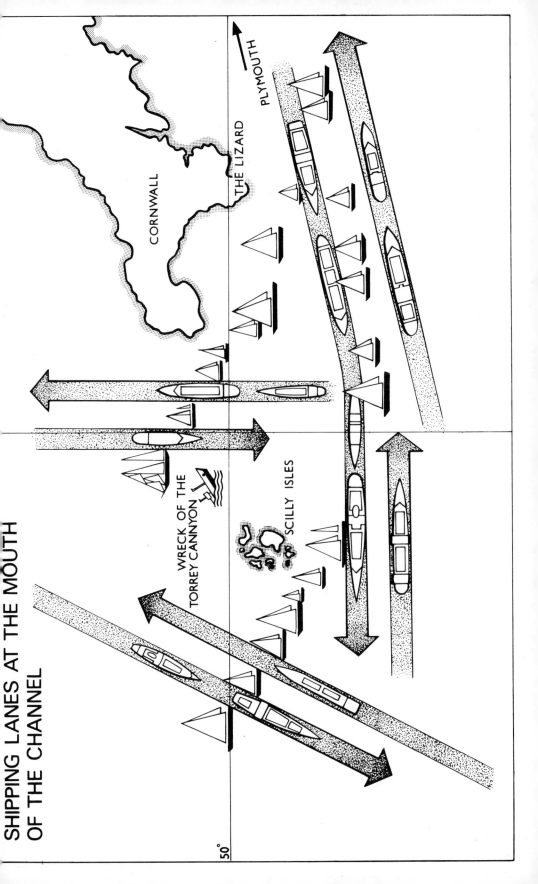

SHIPPING LANES AT THE MOUTH OF THE CHANNEL

CORNWALL

THE LIZARD

PLYMOUTH

WRECK OF THE TORREY CANNYON

SCILLY ISLES

50°

because he will then sleep like a log at the first opportunity. The ability to go without sleep is therefore one of the prime essentials of singlehanded racing, for assuredly the man who spends the most time on deck will be the man who makes the best progress. As the American singlehander, Phil Weld, said before the 1972 race: 'This race has to be won dinghy style, with the skipper always at the helm.' Risk of collision can only be overcome by waking frequently to scan the horizon to spot whether any other vessel is on a converging course. Nonetheless cases of collision do occur, and the many yachts which have disappeared for no apparent reason, have undoubtedly been lost from this cause. This is why the most rigid self-discipline must be practised on board and a routine of broken sleep put into operation as soon as possible, to store up the energy which will be so precious when the wind gets up and sails have to be changed, or when entering busy sea-lanes. Sailing out of the Channel in the early stages of the race demands almost constant watchkeeping. Great care, too, must be exercised when crossing the Grand Banks, remembering the numbers of trawlers fishing there, all totally preoccupied with their work. Making a landfall on America is just as demanding as leaving England, with the added hazard of frequent fogs to complicate the problem. Despite its arduous nature, singlehanded sailing still provides its many practitioners with a fulfilling satisfaction, a feeling of inner peace and an awareness of self-sufficiency, and in this it is a unique sport.

When the singlehanded sailor is asleep he relies completely upon his self-steering gear, which in a very real sense becomes a member of the crew able, in some circumstances, to keep on course as well as any helmsman. But on the other hand many solo yachtsmen have done incredible voyages without it. It has already been noted that Joshua Slocum circumnavigated the world in *Spray* without any such equipment. Of course, he was not racing and could therefore take his time. He had in any case chosen a stable, broad-beamed boat with a hull configuration and sail-plan which enabled her to sail perfectly happily with the tiller lashed. For her day *Spray* was a very fine example of naval architecture. But ocean racing is a very different matter — every minute counts. You have to sail through bad weather carrying sail exactly matched to the yacht's speed potential. The lines of the hull of a racing yacht are much finer than those of a cruising boat and although, of course, the designer never forgets the need for stability his great concern is to minimise the wetted surface in order to reduce drag. Lines such as these make the yachts concerned very tricky to handle and self-steering gear is essential, though in later singlehanded races some modern yachts belonging to very well recognised classes have proved the exception to the rule. But the designer must develop a very close relationship between hull and rig, and stability under way is based upon very special factors.

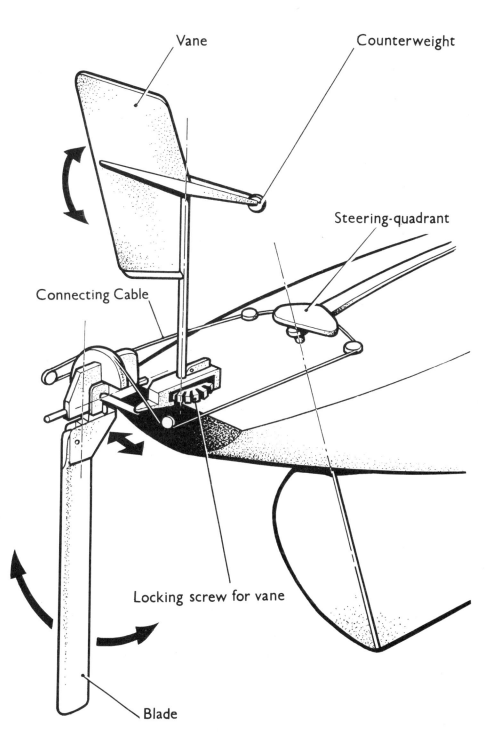

Vane

Counterweight

Steering-quadrant

Connecting Cable

Locking screw for vane

Blade

The American Dick Newick's designs, *Cheers,* and her big sister, *Three Cheers,* have raced in the Singlehanded without self-steering gear, their stability under way being ensured by the balance of hull and sail-plan. However, discussion of these boats must be left for the accounts of the 1968 and 1972 races.

Self-steering gear is set at the stern of the boat and operates on the simple mechanical principle that a vane will always turn to lie along the direction of the wind. The vane acts indirectly through a system of transmission rods and gears upon a blade in the water, so the gear acts as a rudder and sets the boat back on course when it drops away. The vane can also actuate a tab fixed to the trailing edge of the rudder, which moves the latter onto the correct course. A third method — seldom used — is the sail-vane which directly activates the tiller and to do so obviously requires considerable force, so the vane has to be awkwardly large. Such are the three types of gear designed for sailing craft.

Francis Chichester became enthralled by the problem of perfecting his own self-steering gear which he painstakingly built himself. He drew the plans and then constructed a working model in Meccano which caught the imagination of one of his friends who worked for the Sperry Gyroscope Company. Having taken the decision to produce a commercial model, the engineers only discovered in March 1960 that the gear would not work in wind conditions below a certain force. Chichester had to go back to the drawing-board and not until 7 May did the yard finish fitting the gear to *Gipsy Moth.* The yacht was now completely self-steering.

Her wake was almost dead straight. [Chichester wrote] It was fascinating to watch. That was one of the most thrilling moments of my life. Gradually I found out that Miranda, as I had christened the self-steering device, required just as much skill to get the best out of her as does setting the sails of a yacht in a keen race.

The self-steering gear of *Gipsy Moth* was one of the sail-vane type which reacted directly upon the tiller. The sail-vane presented a relatively large area to the wind, so that 'Miranda' was really another miniature sail set in the stern of the boat. Her main disadvantage was her unwieldiness. She suffered in gale force winds and even from particularly heavy seas, and tangled with the shrouds and backstays. None the less she worked well enough to bring Chichester safely home.

Each of the other four competitors were using the same type of gear, with a trim-tab fixed to the trailing edge of the rudder and activated by a vane fixed to the transom. Each successive Singlehanded Race inspired owners to produce their own particular variations of self-steering gear, and this has resulted in the perfection of a number of sound models which have subsequently been produced commercially.

As expected, Chichester made the fastest progress, with Lewis on the same Great Circle route, but some way behind. Hasler set off north-west for the northern course, while Howells and Lacombe were heading far more to the south towards the Azores islands. Howells found that the lashings on his battery had parted and the broken battery had spilled acid over his clothes and food, while Chichester ran into a gale on 25 June which he reckoned at that time had winds of more than 100 mph. 'I hope those other poor devils have not been caught in this', he wrote in his log. 'Personally, I am flogged to the bone.'

Hasler's log reads much less dramatically. He was away up north at 56 degrees of latitude and he wrote, 'In a very boring gale that has been blowing for three days and shows no signs of stopping. I am driving the poor little thing into a filthy breaking sea with four reefs down.' Also bored was Howells. He wrote, 'My mind is boggling at the thought of spending another five weeks in this manner. Have finished all the reading matter—very, very bored.'

By the end of the third week *Gipsy Moth III* was leading the field, about 160 miles ahead of *Jester,* while Howells' *Eira* was far away to the south and now beginning to go well. Lewis was struggling through a belt of calms, while Lacombe had dropped 300 miles behind Howells.

After five weeks Chichester and Hasler were closing the American seaboard, and Christopher Brasher reported in *The Observer* that he expected one of them to finish by the eighteenth or nineteenth. It turned out to be wishful thinking. Meanwhile *Eira* had been knocked flat in a squall when she was close to Bermuda and Val Howells lost his chronometer, so he couldn't fix his longitude. He decided to sail down his latitude to Bermuda, where he arrived at the end of July — and stayed for a week!

When *Gipsy Moth* was a few bare miles from the finishing line she picked up her first landmark, Block Island at the entrance to Long Island Sound. A few hours later Chichester took a number of sightings on the Ambrose Light Vessel and Fire Island to make sure of his position, for visibility was very poor. Then he gave his cabin a tremendous spring-cleaning. At 3.30 pm on the afternoon of 21 July, a fishing-boat came out to meet him. His wife Sheila was on board waving to him, and someone shouted: 'You're first!' and thus Chichester, at the very outset of his career as a seaman, won the first Singlehanded Race in forty days, twelve hours and thirty minutes.

Hasler arrived eight days later, and then Lewis only two and a half days behind *Jester.* As for Howells, the black-bearded Viking, he finished the race in sixty-two days, and, starting five days after the others, Jean Lacombe's *Cap Horn* arrived on 24 August, a seventy-four-days' crossing.

Chichester's log helps us appreciate the physical demands of a race of this sort, even though the boats concerned were easier to handle than those competing in subsequent races. He writes: 'I lost 10 pounds during the race, because, I think, of the big physical effort. Blondie, who said he had done no work at all with his big Chinese sail, also lost 10 pounds. Lewis lost 20 pounds and Howells 18 pounds.'

These figures suitably emphasise the difficulties of an undertaking of this sort which tests to the limits the physique of the men who engage in it. The nervous tension is an abnormally important factor. Lack of sleep for hours and sometimes even for days on end, mounts up to a considerable loss of rest. Meals can never be taken at fixed times and are generally a complete change of diet, and this upsets the system.

The race also makes its demands upon the competitor's mental toughness. Iron self-discipline is needed to solve the host of problems which arise day after day and mile after mile. Nerves of steel are essential to confront the crises which are bound to arise. To be able to do the right thing at the right moment — rapidly — demands enormous reserves, and fear and fatigue must both be mastered. An obstinate endurance plays an enormous part in the life of the singlehanded racing yachtsman and it is this in large measure which forges his seamanship.

The 1960 race provided the first comparisons on the choice of routes. Although the competing boats sailed at different speeds, from that year on it was possible to distinguish the choices for anyone sailing from England to the United States. With each successive race they have become ever more clear, as the other elements emerged, the winds and currents being the most important parameters.

For the inaugural race the competitors had at their disposal the experiences of previous Atlantic crossings as well as the official publications of the various naval hydrographic departments. Most useful of these is the North Atlantic Pilot Chart, surveyed by the US Navy and issued by the Defense Mapping Hydrographic Center in Washington, and this now enjoys a world-wide sale and is used by seamen of all nations. It is in the form of a chart for a given area and is published monthly or quarterly with a certain amount of meteorological information. Charts for the North Atlantic have been appearing at monthly intervals since 1883. Upon it, on a Mercator projection, are to be found a whole host of items of information—principal sea-lanes, depths, direction, force and frequency of prevailing winds, strength and direction of currents, likely occurrence of fog, maximum and minimum extensions of the iceberg zone: in fact, a vast mass of information collected on a single chart, knowledge of which is vital to all seamen. Also charted are the course of depressions (with dates) which have caused recent storms, the positions of weather-ships and the percentage of winds of gale force, while on the back are printed excellent, informative articles on a host of subjects. Singlehanded sailors use this important material as their basic information source. From it they can tell precisely the weather conditions of a given area at the same time the year before.

It can be seen how useful the Pilot Charts are, and yet it must never be forgotten that while situations a year apart may be analogous, they are never the same and can often be very different. It all depends upon the position of the centre of the depression which controls the weather over the North Atlantic, just as the prevailing anticyclone near the Azores governs another area of the ocean. Moreover both weather features are interconnected and one cannot move without the other. Thus, for example, the position of the depression will change the eastward limit of the trade winds.

There is no need to be a professional meteorologist to read the Pilot Chart for June and see that average weather conditions are not particularly favourable for a sailing ship crossing the North Atlantic from east to west. In fact, the strongest winds are west or south-west, Force 3 to 4, at least as far as the Great Circle route between Plymouth and New York is concerned. And here is the crux of the problem for any transatlantic sailor: is it better to sail against the wind along the shortest route, or should he choose a different track, which may be longer but which will bring favourable winds for the greater part of the crossing? Chichester and Hasler chose totally different routes — but then their boats were totally different — so a great deal obviously depends upon the boat chosen as much as on the knowledge and experience of the seaman.

The victor chose a route very close to the Great Circle, which is the shortest route between the starting and finishing points. Lewis, too, adopted the same solution. It totals 2810 miles and passes close off Cape Race, the southernmost point of Newfoundland. Its obvious advantage is its directness. However, it has many disadvantages: first, as previously mentioned, the prevailing winds are 'on the nose'. This means that to have any chance of winning, a yachtsman must have a boat which can sail really close to the wind. Second, the route crosses an area particularly subject to atmospheric depressions, which can be accompanied by gale force winds and heavy seas which can seriously hinder small boats. Other black marks against this route are the difficulties of making a landfall in the persistent fogs caused by the cold Labrador current. However, although the current causes fogs, it flows along Newfoundland and the islands of Saint-Pierre-et-Miquelon in a westerly direction to the advantage of any yacht in it. This is a very important advantage, given that the Gulf Stream, lying slightly further south, runs in an easterly direction that is against any westbound competitor. Finally it should be observed that the Great Circle line runs above the assumed southern limits of the iceberg zone and that thus any boat will have to cross this zone. Despite these disadvantages, the first five Singlehanded Races would seem to show that this is the fastest route. In 1968 and 1972, there were moments when it seemed as if an ultra-light multi-hull would carry off the race by sailing along the southern route, but now this seems far less likely, given the ability of modern trimarans to sail close to the wind. However, in a contest of this sort nothing can be certain.

The Mercator route, which in the North Atlantic lies just to the south of the Great Circle, measures 2920 miles. It cuts the lines of longitude at a constant angle, and is exposed to the same disadvantages as the Great Circle route, and in addition is longer and closer to the Gulf Stream, with its contrary current.

The route taken by Hasler, and bearing his name, takes a wide swing away to the north. It is far longer than the other two, since it measures 3130 miles. Its advantages are the possibility of picking up the favourable Labrador current, and the hope of favourable easterly winds arising from depressions centering to the south of the route. This is, therefore, an attractive course for a boat which sails best before the wind, but it does have the disadvantage of a far greater distance as compared with the Great Circle. And those easterlies are not very reliable.

The Azores route is longer still — 3530 miles — and heads south below the Gulf Stream in search of favourable reaching winds, warmth and sunshine. It could be a very fast route for a multi-hull rigged to run before the wind, but there is a very real danger of extremely light winds over the last quarter of the route. But it is a far more comfortable route than the northern ones. Theoretically it should be unaffected by depressions, but like the trade-wind route it is slightly more in the track of cyclones starting in the Gulf of Mexico and then working north-east. They are, however, few and far between during the summer months.

Further south still is the trade-wind route, a distance of 4200 miles but with the guarantee of favourable winds and fine weather. As it rounds both the Azores and Bermuda it is a very roundabout route with no assurance whatsoever of victory.

The five routes which I have described are not fixed and rigid courses which each competitor follows scrupulously. In fact he will alter his course so as to get the best out of the weather conditions he may encounter. He must therefore have a good knowledge of meteorology. And it is as well to remember Hasler's words: 'so-called prevailing winds have a habit of not prevailing. I don't believe the winds have ever read the American Pilot Charts.'

So the first Singlehanded Race ended in victory for Chichester. It had meant forty days on the toughest route and through fierce storms, the worst of which remained impressed on Chichester's memory:

As soon as I stepped on the deck, I realised that I was in for big trouble. I found a 60 mph wind, which I had not noticed in the shelter of the cockpit, with the yacht bowling down wind. My sleepiness had been partly to blame, but the storm was blowing up fast. . . .

The next morning the wind had dropped. It was still Force 9 but I went on deck relaxed and grateful to be alive.

Such is his description of the worst moment in the race, 25 June, when a storm lasted three days.

Sir Francis Chichester was born in 1901, and by 1960 had already lived a full and varied life. He had been a pioneer airman and had lost count of the number of hours which he had put in on those primitive machines and the number of forced landings which he had made. His enthusiasm for the sea may have come late in life, but by 1931 he was flying a seaplane and this was to make him familiar with the water. The effect of wind speed and direction, the problems of navigation, the study of the various coastlines over which he flew, were all essential elements which were later to help him sail his sea-going *Gipsy Moth*s. He left England for New Zealand at the age of eighteen, where he was to follow a variety of occupations — miner, lumberjack, land agent and publisher. He took his pilot's licence and started an airways firm. From then on he was perpetually engaged on a series of solo flights around the world. In 1929 he became the second man to fly solo from England to Australia. There followed his famous solo flight across the Tasman Sea. After completing his crossing his Gipsy Moth was left at her moorings when one day a sudden gust of wind caused her to founder. The next morning Chichester found her half submerged, but with the help of a mechanic successfully stripped and rebuilt her over a period of months, and took off once more for Australia, which he reached after some hair-raising moments. Later on, and still solo, he flew his seaplane to Japan in an attempt to make a return flight to England via Siberia. Permission was refused for this, but he reached Japan all right. Then there was the accident when his aircraft was being hoisted out of the water by a crane. It nearly cost him his hand but all he lost was one finger. However, the accident he suffered on take-off from the small Japanese port of Katsuura was much more serious. His seaplane hit a high-tension cable and crashed into an outer jetty of the harbour and it was a miracle that Chichester was not killed outright. Nevertheless, his injuries were extremely serious and he was later to admit that it took ten years for him to recover completely from them.

Although I had had a terrific impact with the ground, and could count thirteen broken bones or wounds, I was not seriously hurt. Things like a broken arm and crushed ankle seemed minor troubles. I suppose my damaged back was the worst thing, probably because with the language difficulty the doctor was not aware of it. It was ten years before I was completely recovered from that.

After his return to England, in 1954 and at the age of fifty-three, he discovered sailing. For some time he had known that he was seriously ill, but the flame of adventure burned bright and irresistible. His feats as a seaman match those he performed in the air with his first Gipsy Moth. He has left the memory not merely of a capable seaman in a class of his own, but of a man who above all lived life to its full, even its most hazardous aspects as his subsequent voyages were to show.

RESULTS OF THE OBSERVER 1960 SINGLEHANDED TRANSATLANTIC RACE

START: 11 JUNE

1 *Gipsy Moth*
   FRANCIS CHICHESTER   40 days 12 hrs 30 mins
2 *Jester*
   BLONDIE HASLER   48 days 12 hrs 02 mins
3 *Cardinal Vertue*
   DAVID LEWIS   55 days 00 hrs 50 mins
4 *Eira*
   VALENTINE HOWELLS   62 days 05 hrs 50 mins
5 *Cap Horn*
   JEAN LACOMBE   74 days 00 hrs 00 mins

~~~~~~

CHAPTER FOUR

A Boat Designed for the Race

In 1964 the Royal Western Yacht Club once more organised the race for *The Observer* Trophy. There were far more inquiries from potential entrants than there had been for the first race, but little indication of the growing public interest which the event was to arouse. To broaden the scope and to encourage more boats to enter, the Race Committee decided to create a handicap classification. Later, more subsidiary awards were created. In 1972 came the first competition for the under-35-foot class, while in 1976 there were three separate *Observer* Trophies of equal status for which three distinct classes of boat, of differing lengths, competed. Nevertheless the winner on elapsed time always captures the limelight and this is what makes the race such a success so far as the public at large is concerned.

In 1964 nobody then thought that the North Atlantic could be sailed singlehanded in large boats and when Committee members toyed with the idea of an additional trophy for the best corrected time they turned quite naturally to the RORC to work out the handicap formula. The Royal Ocean Racing Club was born in 1931 from the Ocean Racing Club which had been founded in 1925, the year of the first of the famous Fastnet Races. The dedicated approach of the RORC was soon to make it the arbiter of organised ocean racing with a world-wide following. Once yachtsmen began to go in for racing, they very soon discovered the necessity for a handicapping system which put boats of different size and speed potential on the same footing. Originally they turned to the method employed by the Customs service who calculated length, beam and draught, multiplied them together and divided by 96 to produce the answer in Thames tonnage. Although the old name was kept, very soon handicapping developed principles of its own which basically comprised isolation of all factors favouring the performance of a boat and rating them as penalty points, as for example, length, sail area and stability. Bonus points were given for the factors, such as displacement or weight, beam, and draught, to mention only the most important, which slow the speed of a boat. This handicapping system, perfected by the RORC, has

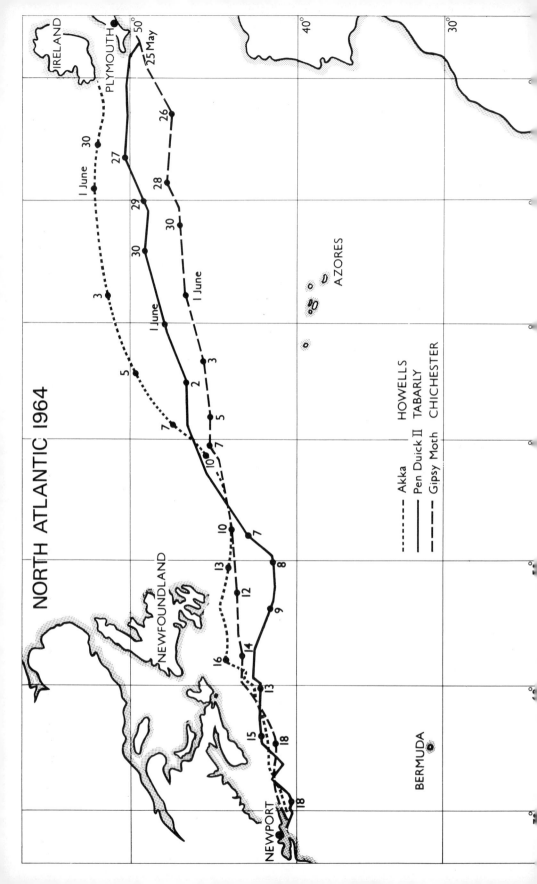

NORTH ATLANTIC 1964

meant that every boat can be given a rating by which the corrected time can be calculated from the elapsed time. In fact the Royal Western Yacht Club was to employ the methods of RORC to calculate the size of each yacht and the handicapping formula they applied was

where L = length.

$$\sqrt{\frac{L + 2}{10}}$$

While the system itself cannot be criticised, the whole idea of handicap classifications may be called into question. Eric Tabarly was among those who drew attention to the possibility of the victor on elapsed time being ousted on corrected time by a boat of lower rating, when to win on elapsed time required far more effort overall. An armchair winner could, he felt, undermine the viability of the race as a whole. But that was really overstating the case, because there was never any suggestion that the handicap winner would outshine the skipper of the first boat home. It is significant that for the 1980 race the committee has dropped the handicap awards, but will give special awards for exceptional passages if it considers any particular boat's voyage has been outstanding. The point is that in singlehanded racing the human factor must predominate. The solo yachtsman has to work himself to the very limit to ensure the fastest passage possible, but he will never achieve the same results as an experienced, full crew. For this reason a handicap based upon the conventional rating principles is a complete gamble. In normal ocean racing the size of the boat determines the size of the crew. Now, although the singlehanded will take steps to modify the topsides and rigging so as to make his boat that much easier to handle, he cannot alter the fact that the bigger the boat the harder it is to work. The best example is the sail area which increases with the size of the boat. If a man is to win on elapsed time, he has to solve a tricky little problem in choosing a boat of the right size to suit his physical capacity and yet capable of the speed he deems desirable. In any case, as we shall see, it is not length which is important but displacement, since this dictates the propulsive power to be generated and hence the amount of sail to be carried.

After the 1964 race the committee decided that the handicaps would not be set according to a formula, but rather to an arbitrary estimate of the time each boat should take to cross the ocean if sailed efficiently by a solo skipper.

For a race like the Singlehanded, I am sure that the proposed restriction on length and the creation of a number of separate categories makes things much more interesting than a handicap system which places all boats whatever their size on the same footing.

Tabarly has suggested that the race should be run by boats with identical hull forms, but with different rigs. This would be an ingenious way of evaluating human performance, since each competitor would choose a sail-plan he himself was able to handle. Chichester too was against the introduction of handicapping, although he recognised that this would make the race far more attractive to owners of smaller boats. In his opinion there simply was no formula which could be applied to single-handed racing. None the less he suggested using as a basis a 9-ton-series boat, which he considered the optimum size, and calculating the rating of the other boats from her. 'Hasler's idea', he wrote in a yachting journal, 'was to plug the gaps in sailing knowledge, and bringing in a handicap virtually obliterates it.' He added: 'Catamarans and trimarans cannot compete in a race decided on corrected time.'

Be that as it may, the handicap rule was introduced for the 1964 Race, although it has never, in fact, been taken seriously by the public at large and the winner of the race won on both elapsed and corrected time.

For the second race the finishing line was altered to run between Brenton Buoy and Brenton Tower off Newport. This did not make much difference, shortening the course by a hundred miles or so, since the start was still from Plymouth Sound, but it did take the finishers away from the crowded shipping lanes around New York.

The five who had competed in the 1960 race turned up again as if by magic. Theirs was no longer a voyage into the unknown, they had not simply read about it, but had gained their knowledge from a battle of forty, fifty or sixty days with the North Atlantic. Four years had passed and this had given time for their experience to ripen. Three of them had different boats, the gear had been rationalised and the rigs better suited to the task in hand. This made the race all that much harder and the competition all the more keen.

At the start there were for the first time representatives of a class of yacht which was in those days the ugly duckling of the yachting world. These were the multi-hulls — two trimarans and a catamaran — which conservatives and traditionalists regarded as dangerous and ungainly craft. This was, in fact, a historic moment, looking back to 1876 when a catamaran, with one of the most famous naval American architects, Nathaniel Herreshoff, at the helm, left 90 mono-hull yachts of the traditional pattern standing in the Centennial Regatta off New York. This was regarded as a joke in very bad taste and the upshot was not long in coming — race committees of the day hastened to bar multi-hulls from competing officially in events under their jurisdiction. However, their sailing efficiency constantly improved until, in 1972, a trimaran was first over the line at Newport in the fourth singlehanded.

Craft of this type are eminently suited to singlehanded sailing and if they did not completely win their spurs in the 1964 race this may be put

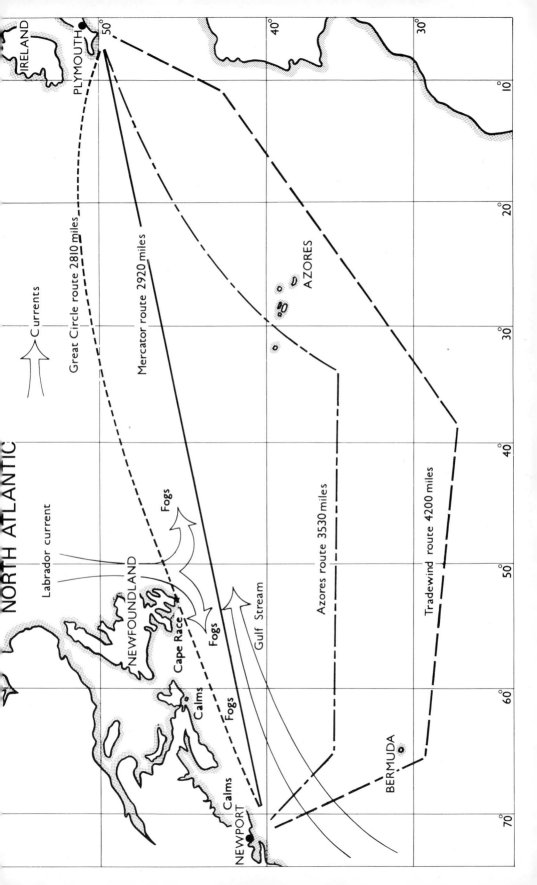

NORTH ATLANTIC

IRELAND

PLYMOUTH

50°

40°

30°

10°

20°

Great Circle route 2810 miles

Mercator route 2920 miles

Currents

AZORES

Azores route 3530 miles

Tradewind route 4200 miles

Labrador current

NEWFOUNDLAND

Fogs

Cape Race

Fogs

Calms

Fogs

Gulf Stream

Calms

Fogs

NEWPORT

BERMUDA

60°

50°

40°

70°

down to the fact that they had not been fully perfected by that time. Why are they so suitable for singlehanded sailing? On their return bygone seamen would describe the graceful manoeuvres of the outrigger canoes seen in the South Pacific and the extraordinary potential of these super-speedy craft. Very few drawings were made of them, the Navy being hide-bound by tradition and against innovation. The whole history of Polynesia is bound up with the study of these craft and they were very definitely multi-hulls in their way.

Weight is the chief enemy of this type of boat, as it is of the singlehanded sailor. The heavier the boat, the more sail it has to carry — a law of diminishing returns for the man on his own. A boat with a light displacement needs less canvas to sail fast. The multi-hull is fast because it is light. Its stability is not based upon the weight of its ballast but upon the way in which its floats are spread out. The drag of the water is very slight, thanks to the boat's lack of ballasted keel. This is a considerable advantage when reaching or running before the wind, but a disadvantage when trying to sail close hauled. For this reason the best multi-hull boats are not usually able to match the best mono-hulls on an east-west Atlantic passage, where the winds are mostly headwinds. But their sailing qualities against the wind have gradually improved and they are now formidable opponents in the singlehanded race. Multi-hull sailors had for so long been content to rely on their boat's speed and to take the longer route in quest of favourable winds, that nobody ever thought they would one day sail the Great Circle route. From 1968 onwards we shall see how close they came to victory, sailing, into the bargain, a course far longer than the Great Circle. And at last, in 1972, a multi-hull won, sailing the Great Circle route.

To return to the 1964 race. Faced by the serried ranks of British yachts, led by Francis Chichester on the same boat which he had used in 1960 and had now refined by another solo crossing (in 1962, taking thirty-three days), the young French sub-lieutenant, Eric Tabarly, decided to develop a boat specifically designed for braving the North Atlantic singlehanded. For the first time a sailing boat was to be built to win the Singlehanded Race. If this seems the obvious thing to do now-adays, it must be remembered that the race was a far less intense affair in those days.

The new *Pen Duick II* soon aroused keen interest in England, where the prospect of strong foreign competition was warmly welcomed. 'Blondie' Hasler told an English journalist on his way to Paris: 'Try to find out all you can about this boat. Real competition from the French is just what we want.' He did not realise how true a word he had spoken.

In those days yacht design had yet to discover many of its refinements. The British, in particular, were traditionally behind the heavy, deep-draught boat, and the sailing qualities of the shallow draught, lighter boat were not yet fully known. In the first place they needed new methods of construction, and to work with new materials and on new lines. In France the Costantini yard at La Trinité had for some time been using marine plywood. The first boat to be built on those lines was *Tarann,* and from her a production boat was developed. Eric Tabarly was an old acquaintance of the Costantini brothers who had helped him restore his first *Pen Duick,* a splendid 10-ton Clyde pilot-cutter designed by the well-known English naval architect, Fife. Thus Tabarly knew precisely how this Breton yard worked.

Towards the end of the summer of 1962, Tabarly made up his mind to enter for the Singlehanded Race in a Tarann. The water-line length was 26 feet and the length overall was $31\frac{1}{2}$ feet. At first sight the length seemed reasonable, since it lay somewhere between the 39 feet of the 1960 winner and the 25 feet of the boat which came in second. An intermediate length was a fair compromise, given that Chichester had sometimes found sail handling too hard. Above all Tabarly was counting upon the light displacement of the boat to give speed and manoeuvrability. Thanks to Commander de Kerviler, then in charge of all sporting activities in the French armed forces, he was posted to Lorient, where he could keep in close touch with the yard. The Costantini brothers offered to build a Tarann at their own expense and lend it to him for the race. They had already called their four successive yachts *Margilic,* and this is why she was christened *Margilic V*. She went on the stocks in 1962 and was launched in April 1963, and the winner-to-be of the 1964 Race trained as a singlehanded sailor and raced with a crew. As his experience grew, so did his realisation that he was so completely her master that he could cope with a bigger boat for the actual race. It was decided that *Margilic V* should be sold and that work should begin on the plans for a new one-off boat. So *Pen Duick II* was born.

Obviously the water-line length was going to be greater than that of *Margilic V,* while holding to the principle of light displacement to avoid a great increase in the sail area which would have to be proportionate to the size of the boat. However, it was now November and *Margilic V* was still looking for a buyer, so Tabarly only managed to get *Pen Duick II* on the stocks in December, when a friend put up the money for her. Work began at once.

Pen Duick II measured 44 feet overall, an 11 feet in beam and was 33 feet on the water-line and this meant that she was a big boat. In normal racing conditions she would need a crew of eight to handle her. In spite of this Tabarly was very confident. Physically, he was stronger than most and he had the temperament of a winner. Few had such a complete experience of cruising and racing under sail. Sailing had always been his sport and his experience with *Margilic V* had given him all the problems of singlehanded sailing to solve. A sportsman and an accomplished seaman, with all the theoretical knowledge and practical experience you could want, he was to go on later to show how right his hunches were about the design of racing yachts. Tough, determined and highly competitive he was a very strong contender indeed in so hard a race as the Singlehanded.

Francis Chichester remained faithful to his *Gipsy Moth III,* the boat he now knew through and through. In 1962 this extraordinary man had set off alone to try to beat his time in the 1960 race and managed to reduce his time of forty days to thirty-three. The experience he gained in so doing was considerable. Although his boat was designed on totally different principles from those of the French favourite, it should not be overlooked that her water-line length was almost the same, though her displacement was greater. From what was known in the months before the race, there was no reason to believe that Tabarly was right. The ability of a light boat to force her way through the heavy seas of the North Atlantic could be questioned, especially when racing against a heavier boat of much the same length. In an Atlantic gale waves may range 20 to 25 feet in height, breaking at the crest. To continue to make way in conditions like those, you need not merely a strong boat but a heavy one as well. Obviously there was going to be a tremendous battle.

Val Howells had changed boats. This time he was racing *Akka* a 35-foot steel sloop designed by the Dutch naval architect, Van de Stadt, and lent to him by a friend. He was to have bad luck, coming into collision with a launch at the start of the race. As a result he lost five hours repairing damage to the boom and self-steering gear, and later had to put in to Ireland to replace a masthead block. He then set off bravely in pursuit.

Colonel Hasler once again entered his junk-rigged boat and remained convinced that the best route was the one which would take him far to the north. There he hoped to pick up the favourable easterlies which would best suit his curious sail-plan.

On the sixth day of the race he had a surprise meeting with another competitor, Alec Rose's *Lively Lady.* She was a cutter of traditional build, 36 feet in length and with 9 tons displacement. At fifty-five, Alec Rose was one of the oldest competitors, but he had had considerable experience of singlehanded sailing in the North Sea, the Baltic, and the Atlantic since selling up his greengrocery business two years before.

David Lewis, an old hand from the 1960 race, had changed boats, but although he raced a catamaran, unfortunately she was too heavy for her sailing performance. She had been ballasted to overcome her instability and this slowed her considerably. Multi-hulls have very little hull area below the water-line and consequently do not take well to overloading. *Rehu Moana* had in fact been built for a planned three-year circumnavigation of the world and not specifically for the Singlehanded Race. The boat was David Lewis's only home now that he had sold his house and left his medical practice.

The fifth competitor to have previously sailed in the race was the Frenchman Jean Lacombe. Once again he was to set sail in the smallest boat to enter: *Golif,* a plastic-hulled sloop from the Jouet yards, measuring 21 foot in length and weighing 2860 lbs. As far as he was concerned, the whole subject of the exercise was to beat the time he had set up in 1960 by taking the shortest route instead of the peaceful track past the Azores which he had sailed before.

Others to represent the multi-hulls were Mike Butterfield's *Misty Miller* and Derek Kelsall's *Folâtre.* The former was forced to put into the Azores for repairs while the latter lost her tiller and a stabilising fin which caused a leak in one of the hulls. As a result she had to put back to Plymouth for repairs. Setting sail once more on 19 June, Kelsall made a passage of thirty-five days to Newport — a good performance.

These are examples of the fragile nature of multi-hulls. They are conceived on lines totally different from mono-hulls and the nature of the stresses placed upon their steering-gear and the crossbeams linking their hulls are still not fully understood. It must be said in their favour that they can move at very great speed, but this is not always sustained because of their light weight. They have little inertia and a heavy sea reacts upon the hulls in a very special way. The port hull does not take the same sea as the starboard hull and the whole vessel is subjected to a torque which places a very heavy strain upon the crossbeams which join them. In fact, the 1964 race was to be the test bench, as it were, for the multi-hulls and the first one in only came seventh. Racing yachtsmen followed the outcome closely and many of them were to gamble on craft of this type in the 1968 race.

Mention, too, must be made of Bill Howell, whose forceful character was to make him one of the leading personalities in the history of the Singlehanded Race. A thirty-eight-year-old Australian dentist from Wimbledon, he had a pretty impressive background under sail, having taken a boat from Europe to Vancouver via Panama and Tahiti. He then bought *Stardrift,* a 30-foot cutter built in 1937, which he sailed singlehanded for the two years preceding the race.

The last four contenders were Mike Ellison in *Ilala* a 36-foot lugsail schooner, built by Nicholson; Bob Bunker at the helm of *Vanda Caelea,* a 25-foot clinker-built sloop; Geoffrey Chaffey in *Ericht,* a 31-foot cutter built in 1938, and Axel Pederson in *Marco Polo,* a ketch with an overall length of 28 feet. The fifteenth entrant, *Tammie Norrie,* scratched. There was every prospect of an excellent race with fourteen contenders, each determined to win.

In the end there were plenty of boats of more than 30 feet, but from the first the forecast had been that, ignoring the multi-hulls whose performance was an unknown quantity, the real battle would be between the holder, Francis Chichester, and the young French challenger, Eric Tabarly. Of course a third boat could always come in out of the blue by choosing a longer but faster route while the two favourites fought it out on the hardest track.

There can be no doubt that both *Gipsy Moth* and *Pen Duick II* were designed for the Great Circle route and the headwinds which sweep it for most of the time. Marin Marie, who has crossed the Atlantic several times singlehanded and whose seamanship is above reproach, expressed his point of view at the time in a yachting journal:

> Admittedly the chances of encountering headwinds are numerous, but taken overall, the proportion of winds which are dead ahead will be less than those coming from the north-west or south-west, allowing the boat to work well to windward to keep on course. And as a good sailing vessel should be able to run close hauled with the tiller lashed, at least in moderate weather, the sailor can take it easy!

The 1960 race had attracted little attention outside the ranks of the few enthusiasts, and they were mostly British. But in 1964 the sailing correspondents of the British national papers were able to stir up more interest and there were regular reports in *The Daily Express, The Guardian, The Daily Mirror,* and, of course, *The Observer.* In France Jean-Paul Aymon of the Paris daily, *France-Soir,* was to follow the race closely, and *Pen Duick*'s victory hit the headlines on both sides of the Channel. Eric Tabarly's character exactly matched the average Frenchman's ideal image of the Breton sailor. In an age of ever-increasing personal frustration one man's feats on the Atlantic kept every French reader on tenterhooks. In specialist circles the progress of *Pen Duick* was followed with considerable interest and respect.

However suitable your boat, you do not simply set out to race across the Atlantic just like that. This is not just a question of winning, but of survival. The boat must be worked up to the pitch of perfection and the sailor's training must be equally faultless, so that he can endure the strain and the sleeplessness and the constant physical effort. Such training will make all the difference between winning or losing, and in certain circumstances between being the master of the situation and going down through failure to do the right thing at the right moment. Of course the singlehander has to sleep, like anyone else, but he has to sleep when it will not upset the handling of his boat.

Each new ocean race also poses new problems of safety at sea. With all the radios in the world nobody can supply immediate assistance over 3000 miles of ocean, and even if a rescue vessel can come to the aid of a boat in trouble, those who have sailed in winds of Force 9 or 10 know just how tricky it is to effect a rescue. Hasler remarked some months before the first race: 'If any singlehander gets into trouble out of reach of rescue, I hope he'll be content to drown like a gentleman.' It is well to remember his words, since they so clearly emphasise that the man in mid-Atlantic can rely on no one but himself.

From the first race in 1960 onwards, the self-steering gear, the singlehander's crewman, was gradually improved. The 3000 miles each competitor had sailed proved its usefulness. With more boats entered and competition that much keener, singlehanders were forced to ask more of their equipment. Choice of well-designed self-steering gear is a prime requirement for winning and we shall see how Tabarly came within an ace of abandoning the 1964 race when his gear developed a defect. However, he went on and won, something very few people could have done and something which makes his exploit unique of its kind. Oddly enough, he was to have an almost parallel experience in the 1976 race.

Chichester reduced the area of his mainsail so as to move the backstay slightly forward and give 'Miranda' plenty of room. As in the first race his gear worked directly onto the tiller.

Pen Duick's gear relied upon a very different system designed by the French engineer, Gianoli. The axis on which the vane turned was not vertical, but at a slant and the angle of inclination was adjustable according to the force which the gear was required to exert. In neutral, as it were, the vane aligned itself with the wind, like any normal self-steering gear. Once it had been engaged it tilted until a balance had been achieved between the force the gear exerted upon the tiller and the far more powerful force exerted by the rudder according to the setting of the gear. This ingenious arrangement, it has been calculated, exerted twenty times as much force for the same area as conventional self-steering gear, although the transmission system was far more complex. Thanks to the great force which it generated, the surface area of the vane was comparatively small and this removed the need for a gear which cluttered up the stern. The principle employed showed great possibilities and, once it had been perfected, the system by which a wind-vane activated a blade below the water-line, a very efficient type of self-steering gear resulted. Tabarly himself met the costs of the research.

Most of the other competitors had conventional gear, comprising a tab on the rudder activated by a vertical shaft to the wind-vane. Self-steering gear is undoubtedly the most sensitive spot on a boat. It needs to be adjusted every time the sails are trimmed and its efficiency will vary from craft to craft. Because of this the interaction of hull configuration and sail-plan must be studied in order to achieve the optimum balance so that the self-steering gear has less work to do. This goes for all yachtsmen, but particularly for singlehanders who rely far more upon the gear.

Start day of the 1964 race was 23 May and this time Plymouth Sound was packed with boats. There were not merely the fifteen competitors at the start, but crowds of spectators aboard all sorts of craft. The British, who have always been sailors, have the happy knack of being able to clamber aboard anything that floats and appear to be perfectly at home on it. They were there in rowing boats, motor cruisers and yachts of every shape and size. Their fleet of small craft was in sharp contrast to the massive three-masted sail training-ship *Danemark,* anchored off Drake's Island, her cadets perched on the topmost yards to watch the start.

Pen Duick II was not ready until the last minute. Tabarly, who had hoped for several months' preparation time to work up the boat, had in fact only had the run between La Trinité and Plymouth to do so. On the eve of the start, painting was still unfinished and the modification of the sails and the search for a log to measure the speed and the run of the boat, took up a great deal of time. The skipper only solved these problems on the morning of the race. He had also to caulk the perspex bubble set in the cabin roof. Tabarly had acquired it in Brittany from a scrap merchant and it had come from an old flying-boat. It enabled Tabarly to keep an eye on the set of the sails while he was under way without having to go on deck. The idea was later to be widely copied, particularly by singlehanders. Indeed the distinguishing marks of modern ocean cruising or singlehanded yachts are the perspex dome and the self-steering gear.

Despite the last-minute rush, *Pen Duick II* had her spinnaker up a few minutes after the starting-gun was fired. The sight will remain engraved in the memories of many and will in some measure be the symbol of the skill and strength of this peerless seaman. The rig had been devised to lessen the surface area of each of the sails, but the 880 square foot spinnaker was still a very respectable size. This large sail is difficult to set because of the number of halyards and guys involved and the singlehander must be perfectly trained to handle it successfully. The rigging must be carefully thought out so that each line leads back to the cockpit and this is particularly true of the halyard which hoists the spinnaker. If this is commonplace nowadays, in 1964 it was still something out of the ordinary. From that moment, those who did not yet know Eric Tabarly were deeply impressed by his speed and determination to snatch every yard in the first few miles of the race. The wind was quite light and blew from astern.

Francis Chichester had perfected a very different rig. He used a pair of twin headsails hoisted on a pair of booms set very high. They had the advantage of keeping *Gipsy Moth* more firmly on course than a spinnaker and of splitting the sail area into two equal and independent halves which made for ease of handling. However, in the hurried moments of the start a spinnaker is a far better investment and *Pen Duick* took full advantage of it. Twin staysails come into their own in a stiff breeze and a rough sea, when it is dangerous to continue to carry a spinnaker, as it can make the boat roll so much that neither the helmsman much less the self-steering gear can control her and the wind may even lay her on her beam ends. In any event the spinnaker forces the singlehander into constant fine adjustments of its trim so that he must be ever on the alert, and it demands strength and dexterity when the time comes to lower it. It is a sail for the enthusiast and while none can deny its advantages for fast running before the wind, to handle it you need to be a good seaman and an acrobat combined and, on some occasions, a trained athlete as well.

Compared with the previous race, the weather for the first few days was pretty fair, a considerable advantage when crossing the commercial shipping lanes. In fact the Channel is always crowded with cargo ships coming in from the Atlantic or the Irish Sea, either to dock in southern English ports or making for the North Sea or the Baltic, and these constantly pass the competitors or cross their bows. There are also plenty of vessels heading out in the same general direction as that taken by the race. It is precisely here that the singlehander needs to keep his eyes open to spot the navigation lights, judge the heading of the vessel concerned and take the necessary avoiding action. For although steam is supposed to give way to sail, the sailor can never be sure that he has been observed and must remain on the alert. Then he must put the helm over, haul in the sheets, watch the port light slowly disappear and the starboard light come into view, waiting with bated breath until he knows that danger is past. Cruising yachtsmen always have some good stories about crossing sea-lanes!

According to Chichester, weather conditions for this crossing were much less severe than they had been in the first race. He did not encounter fog until he reached the Grand Banks off Newfoundland, in other words until he had sailed 2000 miles. In 1960 he had sailed 1400 miles through fog, and he attributed the better average speeds of 1964 to the more favourable weather conditions.

The Englishman's track was slightly to the south of Tabarly's and they sailed parallel courses for the first fourteen days until the latter turned south and they crossed. By that time the Frenchman was four days ahead of *Gipsy Moth,* which on 10 June passed the point which *Pen Duick* had reached on the sixth.

Nevertheless, slightly earlier, on 31 May (that is at the end of the first week of the race) Tabarly suffered a mishap which could have had grave consequences for him. He had already replaced a faulty part of the self-steering gear when, a few days later, taking advantage of calm weather, he decided to oil the mechanism. It was then that he realised he had lost the blade. This caused him momentary anxiety, but remembering he had shipped a spare, he thought he could replace it. Only when he had hoisted the gear aboard and taken it to pieces did he notice that a bolt had sheered and become stuck inside the gear. It refused to come out and there was nothing which he could do to remove it. Now that he could not use self-steering gear, the whole race seemed in the balance. The situation was quite simply catastrophic.

> In such circumstances [Tabarly wrote later] it would have been sensible to give up and cruise the rest of the way to America. Once there, I could have the gear mended and make up my mind what to do next. It was the sensible way out, but it was also the easy way out. I had every excuse on my side . . . But then I thought what a figure I should cut when I got back to France and told my tale of woe to all those who had helped and encouraged me. The least I could do was try to finish the race. It did not matter where I came, the sporting decision to my mind was not to give up but to reach the finishing line whatever it cost. To abandon the race just because you have lost all hope of winning it, simply would not be sporting.

Having decided to carry on, Tabarly now had to work out a means of keeping his boat on course when he left the tiller to get a few hours' sleep. Thanks to the breadth of her beam, *Pen Duick II* was a comparatively steady boat. One thing is absolutely sure: no other boat and no other man could have carried on and have maintained an average daily run which was to bring them both victory in spite of everything. When the weather moderated, *Pen Duick II* ran smoothly on with the tiller lashed. Admittedly, her rudder was set well astern which appreciably increased her lateral plane — the principle factor determining stability under way. None the less when the state of the sea altered or the wind changed, the steering had to be adjusted accordingly. Tabarly was at sea another three weeks and all this time he had to be constantly on the alert. The difficulties he encountered may be imagined.

Although his spirits were unaffected, he believed he no longer had a chance of winning. The time he had lost while he tinkered with the self-steering gear, and the additional loss of time he was bound to incur during the next three weeks gave him little hope of winning on handicap. The tell-tale compass in the cabin roof above his bunk enabled him to check the course when he was half-asleep. The slightest change in rhythm, the slightest deviation from his heading and Tabarly would be out of his bunk. If the weather was cold, he would then have to dress before going on deck. He always wore pyjamas, since in fact he regarded them as the best wear for a decent sleep. In any case his alarm-clock was always set to call him out for regular watches when he would take a look through the perspex dome to make sure that all was well.

His life below decks was simple. As soon as he was able, he would go to sleep on one or other of the pair of bunks, his choice depending upon which way the boat was heeling. Otherwise he would be either in the galley or at the chart table. There was no saloon in *Pen Duick II* and Tabarly had his meals facing his stove, sitting on the wide saddle of a Harley-Davidson motor-cycle, with a strap to support his back when the boat rolled. His chart table was gimballed so he had a level surface to work on and there he worked out his positions from the star or sun sights taken with his sextant. After marking his chart he would then decide on what bearing to sail as prevalent weather conditions dictated. He had plotted a precise course before he started and tried to keep as close to it as the weather allowed. He was helped by forecasts on his radio.

A little further to the north, Chichester was gradually closing the gap between himself and Newport. He went steadily about his daily routine until he noticed that his boat was making a great deal of water. Early on in the race, he knew that he had hit something like a piece of driftwood or floating wreckage, but there had been no serious consequences at the time. When the hull began to leak he gave 1400 laborious strokes to the pump in a single day without lowering the level of water, and he still had not discovered the location of the leak. There was no cause for immediate alarm, but the situation was serious. On 3 June, with a strong wind and a choppy sea, *Gipsy Moth* rode the waves with her canvas reduced to a small jib. Although it was virtually impossible to undertake the smallest task below, Chichester nevertheless examined the hull of the boat, as well as the galley-pump and the stern, to see if he could find where the water was coming in. At noon he recorded a day's run of 110 miles. All this work, prone or doubled up in the bilges, brought on an attack of sea sickness, but at last he could confide to his log that the position of the leak had been discovered in the forward planking. To see better he removed a sliding drawer and peered through. He wrote:

> It was horrible to see water welling out on three sides of this wood block, the leak was worse each time *Gipsy Moth* hit a wave. I was afraid that the planking would come adrift and the Atlantic pour in.
> I had to work with one arm through the hole where the sliding drawer had been. I could only see what I was doing with one eye.

Chichester had taken on board a plate, in case he should need to repair collision damage, and a frogman's suit as well. To fit the plate would have to wait until the seas moderated and once fitted it would

1. Plymouth. Competitors in the outer harbour on the eve of the start.

2. Francis Chichester explains the principles of his self-steering gear (which he christened Miranda) to Eric Tabarly.

3. The peculiar shape of *Jester*. Hasler was to take the northern route.

4. The very individual rig of Mike Ellinson's *Ilala*, with her two junk sails.

5. Geoffrey Chaffey's *Ericht II*.

6. Jean Lacombe's *Golif*. He was out to beat his 1960 time.

7. Bob Bunker on his *Vanda Caelea*.

8. David Lewis's *Rehu Moana*, one of the three multi-hulls entered.

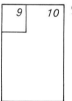

9. Eric Tabarly, winner of the 1964 race, and *Pen Duick II* (10) leaving the start under her spinnaker.

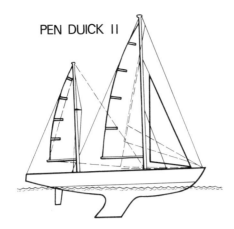

PEN DUICK II

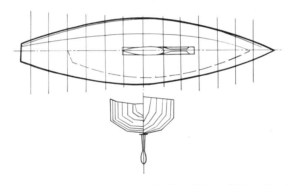

1964—Eric Tabarly—*Pen Duick II*—27 days 23 hrs 00 mins

    Length: 44 feet (mono-hull)
    Hard chine plywood hull
    Ketch-rigged
    Architect: Tabarly-Costantini
    Builder: Costantini (France)

slow the boat considerably and greatly handicap him in the race. So he called up Mashfords yard at Plymouth on the radio to ask their advice. By nightfall, repairs had almost been completed, the hull was no longer making water and *Gipsy Moth* was back to her old speed and racing rhythm. Chichester wrote 'Hurrah! Hurrah!' in his log.

Other competitors had their problems, too. Valentine Howells was assuredly the unluckiest. After the collision at the start, when he lost several precious hours in repairs, a jammed block at the masthead forced him to put in to Baltimore, Cork in Ireland. Leaving on 26 June, he followed the high northern route which Hasler had again chosen. He made excellent time across to the Eastern American seaboard where offshore calms seriously slowed his progress.

Pen Duick II still led the field in winds which were sometimes what seamen would call distinctly fresh. More than once Tabarly was doubled over his tiller running before a squall. With no self-steering gear, he had to take the helm in bad weather and this trapped him in the cockpit for hours on end with no chance to rest or to take food. Changing headsails became a job for an acrobat and he had to pick exactly the right moment to make a dash for the bows to do the deck work. The conditions forced the boat's track southwards. Bad weather and squalls with frequent winds of up to 40 knots made Tabarly take avoiding action and prevented him from getting a sun- or star-fix. Suddenly, on 8 June, the weather cleared and there was *Pen Duick II* sailing in the warm current of the Gulf Stream, which curves up from the Gulf of Mexico, along the seaboard of the United States and then swings away towards Europe. If sailing conditions are distinctly more pleasant in it, the same cannot be said in terms of speed. *Pen Duick II* was now proceeding against a current of at times one knot, which meant that she was losing at least 24 miles every twenty-four hours. However, the Labrador current, although cold, runs inshore of the Gulf Stream down the American coast in a south-westerly direction, and flows at about the same speed the opposite way. Consequently, Tabarly took no time in making up his mind to alter course slightly to the north so as to get out of the Gulf Stream.

This faced him with a fresh problem. All competitors sailing the Great Circle route must beware of Sable Island, of ill-repute since it has caused a couple of hundred shipwrecks since 1800. The causes for this are easy to understand. Ships came near the island after having crossed an entire ocean. Unless they had been able to plot their position accurately within the last few days, they could easily run into this isolated hazard. Added to this poor visibility is an almost constant feature of this area, and currents and strong drift often drive a ship off course.

Tabarly meanwhile was finding it hard to wake up at the right time. First his self-steering gear, then the log which gave him his speed, and now his alarm-clock had packed in — and it was the only one he had taken on board. Then he had a fresh worry. A block at the masthead had worked loose and he was forced to go up to mend it. He succeeded at the third attempt and it cost him a full morning's work. It is hard to visualise the sheer physical effort involved in such an operation. The boat runs with the tiller lashed. As she pitches and tosses in the waves her movements are magnified enormously at the masthead, so these were repairs which needed all his fitness and strength. One false step and Tabarly would have been shattered on the deck more than 40 feet below, or pitched into the sea. But the complicated rigging of the first *Pen*

Duick, which he had had to climb to set the gaff-topsail, had taught him to be surefooted.

But above all the last few days of the race were a strain upon the nerves. The wind was light and very variable, seeming to come from every point of the compass at once, and the boat made slow progress. Fog made visibility extremely poor and Tabarly began to feel very tired indeed. He had not the slightest idea where the other competitors were and he honestly believed that Chichester was ahead of him, since the failure of his self-steering gear had cut down his average speed.

When I thought of all the time which I had lost through countless changes of course, through equipment failing at exactly the wrong moment, through sailing close-hauled half the time with the headings determined more or less by guesswork, I could not help thinking that I must still be far from the finish. I wondered if Chichester was getting close to it. The multi-hulls must undoubtedly have been helped along by following winds, *Folâtre* and *Misty Miller* could reach considerable speed on the open sea.

Throughout the race news arrived regularly at Newport of the progress of Chichester, Lewis and Howells. *The Guardian* published a daily bulletin and issued a little map of the North Atlantic on which the positions of the competitors were plotted. Although Tabarly had tried to establish radio contact with Le Conquet in Britanny on 28 May, he had failed and then had stopped sending out radio messages. His last position had been reported on 4 June by a freighter which had crossed his track.

On 12 June a Canadian Air Force plane reported Chichester 630 miles east of Halifax. At last, on 15 June, another Canadian aircraft sighted the Frenchman about a hundred miles south of Halifax. Thus *The Guardian* made *Pen Duick II* the runaway favourite, although other boats might be closer to the finish since not all the competitors had been sighted. All the same the news was received with some astonishment in Europe, since all along *Gipsy Moth* had been making the headlines, mainly because Chichester was reporting back daily.

At last, on the morning of 18 June, Tabarly sighted the Nantucket Light Vessel anchored on the horizon. It rapidly increased in size, a launch put off from it and a man shouted that there was no one ahead of him. But the Light Vessel marks the shoals lying to the east end of Nantucket Island so competitors could have passed to the south without being seen by the watchkeepers.

This was the first mark Tabarly had sighted since leaving England astern. Although Texas No 2 Tower, guarding the Georges Bank, should have been on his track, he never saw it. It was only later that he chanced to hear it had been recently destroyed.

Light winds were a feature of those last few days. Aircraft escorted *Pen Duick II* while Tabarly started his last sleepless night. The next morning a launch cut across the bows of the French yacht and in it Tabarly was amazed to discover his aunt, who called to him that he was leading, two days ahead of Chichester.

> It was hard for me to grasp the idea. I must have lost rather less time than the others and the failure of my self-steering gear may have been a blessing in disguise since it forced me to keep a constant lookout. I think, too, that I was lucky to have a fast boat and one which was easy to handle.

When Chichester heard that Tabarly had won in twenty-seven days, he confided to his log the question which anyone would have asked himself, Could I have done better? News of the Frenchman's success had taken him by surprise, but he acknowledged that Tabarly's seamanship, racing skill and stubborn endurance made him a well-deserving winner. Chichester genuinely admired his rival's feat and felt that it had been a privilege to race against both him and *Pen Duick II*.

When *Pen Duick II* crossed the finishing line, *Gipsy Moth* still had another 268 miles to go and Chichester still had two days and twenty hours in hand to achieve his heart's ambition — of finishing in under thirty days. The following night, Chichester spent plenty of time on deck taking avoiding action while ships seemed to come at him in all directions. He was to learn later that he had run through a fishing fleet of two hundred and eighty Russian trawlers!

Chichester was quite overcome when he crossed the finishing line by the Brenton Light Vessel, just three minutes under thirty days. He relinquished his title to Tabarly, but finished a brilliant second, realising his dream of breaking the thirty-day barrier. Typically, he then had his green dinner-jacket cleaned and repaired, all ready, he hoped, to be worn four years hence for the third race in 1968.

The wisdom of age yielded to the physical strength of the young athlete who was soon to become so famous. They were both matchless seamen, as they were subsequently to prove still further by the extraordinary voyages each was in his own way to make across the oceans of the world.

Despite all his difficulties at the start, it was Valentine Howells who was to take third place in *Akka*, helped by those easterlies up on the northern route. He finished four days ahead of *Lively Lady*. Alec Rose's cutter had had a comparatively easy run, the worst moments were winds of over Force 9 in mid-ocean and the pitiless calms of the last week. Two sorts of weather condition so utterly different and yet so typical of the race. In fact, they make it the tough event it is.

Hasler remained faithful to his northern route and finished fifth, cutting ten days off his 1960 time in the same boat. His most vivid memory was the sight of a gigantic iceberg rocking in the green swell with the white foam breaking against it.

The multi-hulls came in seventh, eleventh and thirteenth respectively. *Rehu Moana* took the shortest route and survived the 60-knot winds which she encountered. Unfortunately the self-steering gear failed and David Lewis had to spend most of the race at the helm.

Misty Miller chose the southern route and was forced into the Azores for repairs, while *Folâtre* having put back to Plymouth to mend her rudder only got away again on 19 June. She reached Newport on 24 July.

Jean Lacombe, the second Frenchman in, had entered the smallest boat. He finished ninth having made a very good average speed along the Great Circle, a particularly difficult route for a boat as small as his. Like the other competitors, he encountered extremely bad weather in the North Atlantic from 4–10 June, lost his main boom and had to replace it with a spinnaker pole. Mike Ellison's *Ilala* lost her mizzen-mast and finished the race under jury rig.

But *Pen Duick* made light of all the dirtiest tricks the race could play. And there were plenty of them, as a glance at the difficulties encountered by the other competitors will show. Force 8 and 9 winds are all too frequent along the Great Circle track and calms are just as likely to hinder the maintenance of a good average speed, especially near the finish. The more closely the conditions under which the race is run are examined, the stronger grows the realisation that it is truly a unique contest. The race can only be won by an all-weather boat, which can ride the westerlies and still make headway in the light winds on the last 800 miles from Newfoundland.

For these reasons Tabarly had been most farsighted in conceiving a boat admirably designed to sail close hauled in rough seas, yet with a comparatively light displacement which made her easier to handle and more efficient in light winds. His solution was the hard chine hull built of marine ply, which combined strength and lightness. Meanwhile the ketch rig split the total sail area into as many component parts as possible without loss of efficiency. For this reason the mizzen was set as far astern as possible so as not to interfere with the mainsail, but to give room for an effective mizzen staysail. The wide spread of the sails contributed also to the stability of the boat. The forward sail-plan was split in two, as well, between jib and staysail. These are the two easiest sails to handle and while one is being changed the other continues to draw. The space between them forms a slot which makes the staysail more efficient, and last but not least, because this sail needs an inner forestay the mast is more strongly supported.

And the key to Tabarly's success was that his boat had been designed especially for the race. Original as they were for the time, the ideas behind the design of such a boat proved to be well-founded and the mark of very shrewd judgement.

Tabarly's upbringing explains in part the demands he makes not only upon others but most of all upon himself. Although an innovator by temperament, he is by no means closed to traditional influences. When he won the race he was a thirty-three-year-old Lieutenant in the French Navy. A veteran naval pilot with plenty of experience in Vietnam, then known as French Indo-China, he passed through the Naval Staff College and was posted to the minesweeper flotilla at Cherbourg. His naval career did not stop him sailing whenever and wherever he was able.

After 1965 he was seconded from the Navy to the Ministry of Sport and is at present stationed at the Inter-Service Sports Centre, Fontainebleau, where he is in charge of ocean sailing.

Tabarly was welcomed at Newport as the victor. His exhausted, but deeply happy face, with its scrubby beard, made the front pages of the world's press.

In France the news was in all the headlines. Here was a man who had not only conquered the Atlantic singlehanded but had into the bargain beaten the English at their own game. No wonder he quickly became a popular hero!

His victory was to have considerable repercussions in France, not merely for sailing itself, but in popularising the sport. The closed circle of racing yachtsmen was to widen and this had its impact upon the boating industry as a whole. The victory helped to advance the technique of fitting and rigging small boats. Meanwhile the audience for the race started to interest major manufacturers who began to have an inkling that their products could be pushed by the publicity this event attracted, and four years later the third race brought the word 'sponsor' into sailing.

Pen Duick II returned to Britanny. She received a triumphal welcome as she made her entry into port late one morning at the height of the holiday season, with all the yachts blowing their foghorns and the cars on the quayside hooting like mad. Tabarly was back in the harbour he had left a few months earlier for Plymouth, and he picked up his moorings close to the Costantini yards where his boat had been laid down.

In January 1965, visitors to the Paris Boat Show were able to admire the amazing black ketch which was exhibited for six days in the heart of the capital. Tabarly was happy, and if he enjoyed the honours paid him, his friends knew that they did not go to his head. His thoughts were more on the possibility that a singlehander could take an even bigger boat across the Atlantic.

In Washington, the French Ambassador to the United States, Monsieur Hervé Alphand, had, in the name of the President of the French Republic, presented the naval Lieutenant with the cross of Chevalier of the Legion of Honour for his 'outstanding feat'. On 24 November he received from the hands of the Chief of Defence Staff, Lord Mountbatten, *The Observer* Trophy in London. When he reached France, Maurice Herzog, Secretary of State to the Ministry of Sport, was there to greet him. For the winner, his victory was merely a step, an important step of course, in his search to improve his performance and to achieve ever greater speed under sail. Those who seek a justification for entering the race, should remember the closing words of Tabarly's book:

This race has the virtue of being contested for its own sake. It is its own justification as are the mountaineering expeditions which some people say are a waste of time. I think that the personal satisfaction felt by mountaineers at the end of a successful climb is justification enough. The same thing goes for the Singlehanded Race and for the same reason it deserves to be regularly contested.

RESULTS OF THE 1964 SINGLEHANDED RACE

START: 23 MAY

		Elapsed Time	Corrected Time	
1	*Pen Duick II*			
	ERIC TABARLY	27 days 03 hrs 56 mins	21 days 23 hrs	1
2	*Gipsy Moth III*			
	FRANCIS CHICHESTER	29 days 23 hrs 57 mins	22 days 18 hrs	2
3	*Akka*			
	VAL HOWELLS	32 days 18 hrs 08 mins	24 days 07 hrs	3
4	*Lively Lady*			
	ALEC ROSE	36 days 17 hrs 30 mins	27 days 09 hrs	5
5	*Jester*			
	BLONDIE HASLER	37 days 22 hrs 05 mins	25 days 04 hrs	4
6	*Stardrift*			
	BILL HOWELL	38 days 03 hrs 23 mins	27 days 12 hrs	6
7	*Rehu Moana*			
	DAVID LEWIS	38 days 12 hrs 04 mins		*
8	*Ilala*			
	MIKE ELLISON	46 days 06 hrs 26 mins	34 days 20 hrs	9
9	*Golif*			
	JEAN LACOMBE	46 days 07 hrs 05 mins	30 days 00 hrs	7
10	*Vanda Caelea*			
	BOB BUNKER	49 days 18 hrs 45 mins	32 days 22 hrs	8
11	*Misty Miller*			
	MICHAEL BUTTERFIELD	53 days 00 hrs 05 mins		*
12	*Ericht 2*			
	GEOFFREY CHAFFEY	60 days 11 hrs 15 mins	42 days 23 hrs	10
13	*Folâtre*			
	DEREK KELSALL	61 days 14 hrs 04 mins		*
14	*Marco Polo*			
	AXEL PEDERSON	63 days 13 hrs 30 mins	44 days 21 hrs	11

* No corrected time for multi-hulls

CHAPTER FIVE

The Triumph of Planning

Tabarly had set the tone. If anyone wanted to be up among the winners in 1968, they could no longer enter just any boat. The widespread interest which the 1964 race had aroused, had resulted in a number of inquiries for entry forms and potential competitors had had four years to think things over. The third race held every promise of excitement from the numbers entered and from their quality. The advance in the performance of multi-hulls was a strong card and the wide variety of types of boat entered made it a particularly open race.

The Singlehanded Race had come of age and had become a race of prime importance. However, the small proportion of finishers to starters was going to raise fundamental questions. In 1960 all the entrants had reached the finishing line; in 1964, although some competitors were forced in for repairs, they all got under way again, and only one of the fifteen retired. But in 1968 it was to be a massacre — only nineteen of the thirty-five boats which left Plymouth reached the finish and the other sixteen were ruled to have retired for various reasons. In three cases they sank and their skippers were only saved by good fortune, fortune which involved the resources of the rescue services in both men and materials for several days. Although the rules had been tightened up since 1964, it looked very much as if the Race Committee was rather more soft-hearted in applying them. On the other hand, it must be said that weather conditions were far from favourable.

To be an official finisher in the 1968 race you had to make a passage of under sixty days. This rule eliminated at a stroke some very small boats. If it had been applied in 1964, for example, only eleven boats would have been finishers. Failure to complete in sixty days, kept the entries down by cutting off the bottom of the list.

The second and much more important new rule required every entrant to have sailed a qualifying 500 miles singlehanded cruise. This rule was designed to eliminate incompetent entrants right from the start. You would think that unless you were experienced enough to get across the Atlantic singlehanded you would keep well away from the race, but,

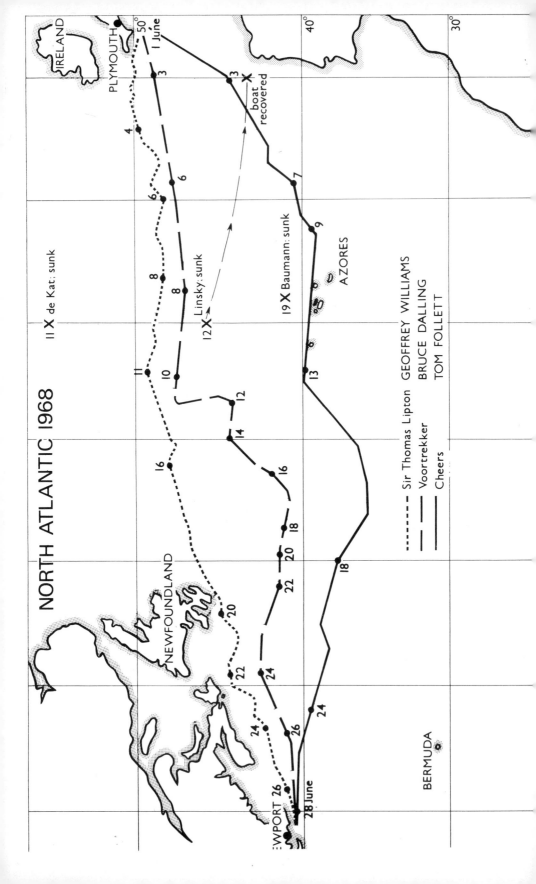

NORTH ATLANTIC 1968

IRELAND

PLYMOUTH

50°

1 June

40°

30°

boat recovered

X

11 X de Kat: sunk

Linsky: sunk
12 X

19 X Baumann: sunk

AZORES

NEWFOUNDLAND

BERMUDA

EWPORT 26

28 June

Sir Thomas Lipton   GEOFFREY WILLIAMS
Voortrekker   BRUCE DALLING
Cheers   TOM FOLLETT

as we shall see, this was not the case and there were people who entered blissfully ignorant of what it was all about.

In a contest of this sort it is essential that the participants take their own safety precautions or else the Race Committee will be overwhelmed by a host of problems which are really not its responsibility. In cases of dire necessity, official organisations can come to their assistance, but competitors ought not to rely upon them.

The wisest precaution was to scrutinise each boat before the start, and if stipulating a qualifying 500 miles was any good at all, so was a safety inspection.

The eventual winner, Geoffrey Williams, was himself to incur a twelve-hour penalty for failing to report to the scrutineers at the time and place specified. This was a typically British decision but was, by chance, given against the most meticulous and best prepared of the competitors.

Francis Chichester gave the 1968 race a miss. He had just completed another outstanding voyage as a singlehander. Having failed to fly round the world as a young man he simply decided to sail round it. While crossing the North Atlantic in 1962 in a successful attempt to beat his own record in *Gipsy Moth III,* Chichester had realised that there was another exciting way to get round the world solo:

As the years passed, this urge to circle the world alone lay dormant in me, like a gorse seed which will lie in the earth for fifty years until the soil is stirred to admit some air, or light, and the seed suddenly burgeons. And so it was with me, only flying, meanwhile, gradually lost the attractions of pioneering to become a matter of technical training and piloting expertise, and all the places I had hoped to go to, where an aeroplane had never been, not only had seen aeroplanes, but had grown used to them, and the usage of them.

So he determined to lay down a new boat designed to sail round the world. He planned only one landfall, at Sydney. John Illingworth's *Gipsy Moth IV* was a very big boat for a singlehander. She measured 54 feet and turned out to be not that well adapted for singlehanded sailing. The old 'British Lion' left Plymouth alone towards the end of August 1966 and reached Sydney in December. Modifications were made to his boat and he set off once more in January 1967. He completed his voyage of circumnavigation in two hundred and twenty-six days. Only in 1970 did he lay down a new vessel with other voyages in mind, including the 1972 Singlehanded Race.

In fact only two of those who had competed in 1964 were to enter for the third race. They were Bill Howell and Eric Tabarly, both in different boats and what is more both in multi-hulls. That old faithful *Jester* was there again, but with Michael Richey at the helm this time and not 'Blondie' Hasler. Since 1964 Tabarly had been getting in the mileage on all the oceans of the world. In this he was like Chichester, but very unlike him in that the Frenchman had been doing it — ocean racing, with a crew. During 1964 *Pen Duick II* competed in a number of RORC events in European waters thus enabling the owner to match his speed with some of the best ocean racers of the day. Since it was his intention to build another boat Tabarly used this opportunity to experiment with a new schooner rig and to test out its efficiency. He then changed the boat back into a ketch but kept the wishbone yards on the mainmast, having in mind the Newport-Bermuda Race which started in June 1966. The hull had also been slightly modified to satisfy American rating rules and the stern shortened. Tabarly sailed her singlehanded across the Atlantic via the Azores to the start, where his crew met him.

In May 1967 *Pen Duick III* was launched. She was a respectable size, measuring 43 feet on the water-line and 57 feet overall. She had been built to RORC rating rules and was intended for racing in British waters in 1967. The British will long remember her! She took first place in her class after a run of wins on both elapsed and corrected time. Her schooner rig will go down in the history of the RORC and her splendid lines will remain fixed in the memories of many ocean racing enthusiasts.

Tabarly went on notching up the miles and the experience. *Pen Duick III* took part in the Sydney-Hobart Race at the end of December 1967 and then cruised the Pacific for several months. But his eyes were still firmly fixed on the Singlehanded Race. He was beginning to have *Pen Duick* well under control now and her rigging could be simply altered to make her easier to handle singlehanded. But the more he thought about it the more formidable he realised the multi-hulls would be. In September 1967, he had asked the naval architect, André Allègre, to consider the problem. Instinctively Tabarly's preferences inclined towards a trimaran, for safety reasons since catamarans capsize far more easily. Plans for a 66-foot trimaran went on the drawing-board. When he came back from Australia it was time to resolve the problem and after lengthy discussions and much tank-testing, work on the giant craft began. The strikes that broke out in France during 1968 did not help at all and in the end *Pen Duick IV* was only launched on 11 May.

In order to be sure that the huge trimaran was faster than the schooner, Tabarly raced them against each other, and his choice settled firmly for the trimaran, although she was far from being worked up. The most difficult problem was to get peak efficiency from the self-steering gear since the high speeds of multi-hulls created complications which were still imperfectly understood at that time. Nor had there been time properly to test the rotating masts, although they had demonstrated how exciting was the technical principle behind them. The start was from Plymouth on 1 June and *Pen Duick* had had no trials at all to speak of. Thus Tabarly realised just how hard it was going to be to take a boat of such revolutionary design to Newport without running into trouble.

All the same it had been a great step forward and later on *Pen Duick* was to show just what a fantastic boat she was. The concept behind her design was a milestone in the history of sail and she was to become one of the leading ocean-going multi-hulls in the world. One of *Pen Duick's* chief peculiarities was the bulk of her floats. Given the all-up weight of the boat and the considerable distance between the centre of gravity in the central hull and the centre of buoyancy in the windward float, a pair of equal and parallel forces is set up acting in opposite directions and tending to capsize the boat. On *Pen Duick* this capsizing moment is a force of 25 metric tons. The cubic capacity of the floats was deliberately restricted to 5000 litres, so that at the instant when the boat reacts to the capsizing moment and begins to pivot round the float upon which the weight of the boat is exerted the latter is buried in the water, and when it is at 90° from the horizontal, the trimaran simply lies on her beam ends like any ballasted yacht. Were the floats to have a greater buoyancy the weight of the boat would push it further along the arc of the circle and the trimaran would turn turtle. The whole concept of this giant racing machine is extraordinary enough and the victory of Alain Colas, who took her over in 1972, was to prove that Tabarly would have been four years ahead of his time if only he had had a few months to work the monster up to racing pitch.

To build a boat like that costs a considerable sum of money. It could only be undertaken thanks to substantial financial backing, underwritten by signed contracts with the news media, and Radio Luxemburg, *Paris-Match* and *France-Soir* signed for Tabarly's exclusive story of the race. The £35,000 raised by this means may not have been enough to finance the whole operation, but it went a long way towards it. Because of the size of some of the boats entered and the impact it was bound to have upon the public, the 1968 race was the first in which financial problems, contracts and backers were discussed openly.

Pen Duick IV had to abide by specific contracts and the granting of certain exclusive rights, whereas other boats had been entered with the backing pure and simple of the company whose name they carried. Advertising agents handling major accounts had realised the impact the name of a product would have if it were painted on the stern of the winner of something as popular as the Singlehanded Race. The space the press had begun to devote to the race and the noise it made while doing so were worth a well-run advertising campaign. If the operation carried some very real risks, the advertising fall-out helped to put a client's name across. A yacht raced singlehanded across the ocean made a very good trade mark. Thus the advertising industry enabled a number of worthy competitors to put their ideas into practice and to realise their dream of building a boat tailor-made for them. In the third race, then, financial backing was to be found from those great British brewers, Courage, Barclay, Simmonds and Watney-Mann, and from the distillers Cutty Sark and Asti-Gancia, Lipton's the grocers, and from the holiday resort of Saint-Raphaël, as well as newspapers and radio stations.

Although some people may deplore the introduction of such methods into so traditionally based a sport as sailing, it must be remembered that commercial sponsorship has allowed events to be held which have aided research and worked for the long term benefit of sailing. The problem is not to let the money take precedence over the event which it is supposed to support. For top sportsmen it must be the means and never an end in itself.

In 1968, the help provided by Lipton's made Geoffrey Williams the winner. Their sponsorship was very sensibly given. Without it, Williams' boat would have been much smaller and the young Englishman would never have won the Singlehanded Race. With it he was able to give his character full play, and to show the worth of his courage and his meticulous attention to detail. There are many points of interest in the steps which a comparatively inexperienced sailor took to get himself to the starting line on a boat measuring 42 feet on the water-line and 56 feet overall.

Geoffrey Williams was not one of those champions who was born on a boat. It was not until he was nineteen that he first went sailing and from then on he devoted his time to studying all the yachting magazines he could lay hands on. After taking his degree at Oxford in 1965, he went to the United States and taught geography at Saint Bernard's School, New York. During this period he sailed in the West Indies where he chartered a boat. In 1966, during a brief holiday in the country he discovered Eric Tabarly's book *Lonely Victory,* and its account of the 1964 race. He was enthralled by the Frenchman's daring and was immediately drawn by the lure of singlehanded racing.

In the grime, the traffic congestion and the concrete chasms of New York I came to know that I no longer wanted to go cruising — now I wanted to race my own boat! Equally, the Singlehanded Transatlantic Race seemed a much more direct and honest way of working out my bizarre emotions than my devious designs on the Caribbean!

At one time Williams had had the idea of starting a chartering business in the West Indies.

At the time when he decided to prepare for the race, *Pen Duick III* was showing herself to be one of the best boats then in British waters and Williams wrote to six naval architects asking them to design a vessel which was slightly bigger. The only answer which gave him any hope was from the noted English architect, Robert Clark, who was to play an important part in Williams' life, not merely on account of the boat which he designed but because of the mass of advice he lavished on him. It was Clark who suggested obtaining commercial backing right from the start. Because sponsorship inevitably entails publicity, the idea was hardly of the kind to appeal to Williams. 'My reasons for entering the race were personal and introverted and I wanted to leave Plymouth unseen sailing an unknown boat without any sponsored ballyhoo.'

Although Clark had no specific sponsor in mind, he was able to persuade Williams to use a friend of his, a London advertising agent, to look for the money. From then on Williams built up massive files on all aspects of yachting, visited the yards where Derek Kelsall had built the winner of the 1966 Round-Britain Race, *Toria,* and taught himself draughtsmanship in his New York apartment. In the spring of 1967 he began his physical training, walking long distances and running in all weathers.

However, there was not the slightest glimmer of financial backing. He wrote to the Royal Western Yacht Club to get their views on the ethics of advertising sponsorship, should he obtain it. The answer came back that the Race Committee had nothing against that sort of thing, provided the advertising was kept within the bounds of good taste! In the first half of 1967, Geoffrey Williams must have written three thousand letters in the hope of finding the finance which would enable him to increase the length of the boat which he had ordered from Robert Clark from 43 feet to 60 feet.

About this time the idea of having computer assistance for the race began to germinate in his brain. He got in touch with the English Electric Company and they were ready to consider his suggestion. A computer could help him set his daily course by analysing the weather forecasts.

In the end, the board of Allied Suppliers, the company controlling Lipton's, agreed to sponsor the undertaking. Williams had thought of them at the last moment and they had agreed within a week of having his request. In 1898 Sir Thomas Lipton, the founder of the firm, had first challenged for the America's Cup with his yacht *Shamrock I,* a boat nearly 130 feet long. Five *Shamrocks* in all were to be built to challenge for the America's Cup but, magnificent racers though they were, they never overcame the Americans.

From then on Williams had to get down to serious training and during that season took part in many RORC events as a crewman on different boats. He also opened a file on weather conditions in the North Atlantic and analysed conditions for June over the past thirty-five years.

He reached the same conclusions as those which had brought Tabarly to design a light boat which would sail close to the wind. Four years later, although the basic principles were the same, experience had shown that length could be the most important factor. Geoffrey Williams and Robert Clark considered that a glass-fibre foam sandwich hull would be best for her size.

With the help of Derek Kelsall and a friend, Williams built his boat's hull in six weeks. During the winter he continued his training runs and to harden himself to the cold wore the minimum of clothing. On 13 March the hull of *Sir Thomas Lipton* took the water and ten days later the keel was fitted. Finally, on 30 March 1968, Mr Snelling, who had sailed on the last *Shamrock* of the series, despite his ninety-one years, christened the yacht. There remained a few months to prepare her.

Williams' first experience of singlehanded sailing was aboard the boat which he was going to race across the North Atlantic. He completed his 500 miles off the south coast of Britain with no trouble apart from the jib halyard jamming at the masthead. He only managed to clear it on his return to port. The computer system which the future winner had dreamed up some months before was ready and working before the start and monopolised the time of what amounted to a small team who devoted themselves to it both before and during the race.

Weather forecasts for the mid-Atlantic are not detailed enough to give competitors an accurate picture of the day-to-day conditions they are likely to encounter. Williams' system linked him to an English Electric computer, which analysed the weather maps in London and selected the best routes for the conditions. The information was then radioed to *Sir Thomas* every morning.

The 1968 rules had not been drawn up with a navigational aid of this sort in mind, and after the race was over such bitter argument was aroused that any system of pre-arranged information flow was banned. Williams was the only competitor to use such an aid. Present rules forbid outside assistance — in other words the system employed by Williams in 1968 — since to some degree the boat is under remote control from the land. Had this decision not been taken, it would be easy to imagine a future race in which the skipper merely acted as a robot, no longer responsible for the navigation, whether that comprised choice of route or analysis of weather conditions. This would remove a major responsibility from the seaman's shoulders, and diminish greatly the worth of the race in which the singlehander must be helmsman, seaman, crewman and race tactician at one and the same time. If there is some justification in considering that the computer assistance took some of the gilt off Williams' victory, it was still necessary to get the system working. And race preparation, in all its petty detail, is a vital factor — the factor which produced a very different sort of winner from those of the first two races. The first tests with the English Electric computer went back to June 1967 and Williams' victory was built on scientific principles and his training was completed in a similar manner.

In fact the instrument was to play a very important part as will be seen when the race itself is described. It was to allow Williams to forecast the approach of a very deep depression in time and consequently to take the right decisions while all the other competitors sailing the Great Circle route were to suffer considerable delay from it. This was one of the reasons he won.

Among the other thirty-five entrants there were large yachts on classic lines which were to make life hard for *Sir Thomas Lipton*.

On the French side, Alain Gliksman, then chief editor of a yachting journal and a well-known ocean racer, had had a 57-foot aluminium ketch specially built for the race. He was one of the men behind the victory of *Alcatraz* in the RORC championship and was widely experienced in ocean racing. He commissioned the design of his boat from the Marseilles naval architect, André Mauric. She was an elegant yacht, built for the shortest route, with a heavy keel to enable her to sail close to the wind. A generous beam, a hard chine hull, sail-plan and lines all made for a very stable boat, and though from her very size she was something of a handful, she seemed to be particularly suited to singlehanded sailing in the North Atlantic. Alain Gliksman had always been a passionate devotee of the race. He was one of the few French journalists at the start of the 1960 event, and had been on *Pen Duick II* until ten minutes before the start in 1964. As a working journalist he could legitimately keep himself completely informed about the other competitors, and the equipment in his boat was the best available. Thanks to the publicity director of the town of Saint-Raphaël, who intended to use the boat after the race and its advertising value during it, he had a remarkable boat at his disposal. Unfortunately there were serious delays in the building and completion, and working up took place in the chaotic conditions of May 1968 when the strikes brought whole sectors of industry to a standstill. The two months spent preparing for the race at Le Havre, where a small team worked like beavers to get the boat ready, were too short to iron out all the snags. For one thing much more time should have been spent testing the self-steering gear, which was to be one of the reasons why the boat retired, after being one of the front runners for three-quarters of the race. The gear was of the same type which caused *Pen Duick IV* so much trouble and which forced Tabarly, too, out of the race. Still, *Raph* was at the start, and was one of the best-looking boats — to all appearances the best equipped to win at least the mono-hull class.

Voortrekker was undoubtedly one of the lightest ocean racers for her size, displacing 6.3 tons for an overall length of 49 feet. Designed by the naval architect Van de Stadt for the South African, Bruce Dalling, she had a very deep keel, making her a very stiff sailer which gave maximum efficiency when sailing close to the wind. She was ketch-rigged, with a minute mizzen whose only job was to balance the mainsail. Given the knowledge of yacht design available in 1968, she seemed a boat ideally suited to the type of sailing for which she had been built.

The real problem when a traditional yacht of this type is being sailed solo is to know whether it is better to enter a very large boat and use only sixty per cent of her potential sail area or enter a smaller boat and use seventy-five per cent. In any case complete reliance could be placed upon Bruce Dalling's competence, his familiarity with his boat and her race worthiness, since he had had to complete a 5000 mile voyage to bring her from Capetown to the start at Plymouth. It was an interesting boat with a modest and formidably efficient skipper.

Another fancied contender was Leslie Williams, a lieutenant in the Royal Navy, although his *Spirit of Cutty Sark* was not particularly suited to singlehanded sailing. She was a large 53-foot sloop, also designed by Van de Stadt, and her single mast gave the genoa headsail a very considerable area which a lone sailor would find hard to keep safely set for maximum efficiency.

Other 1968 entries included Brian Cooke in *Opus,* a sloop only 32 feet in length and designed on traditional lines. Considering the size of his boat, Cooke achieved a remarkably high placing, coming in sixth on elapsed time and third on handicap (multi-hulls being excluded from this classification).

Mention of Brian Cooke brings to the forefront one of the tragedies of singlehanded sailing, for Cooke was lost at sea on the eve of the 1976 Race in his 46-foot trimaran, *Triple Arrow.* Her skipper had last been heard of early in the year in the Atlantic trying to set up a singlehanded record for an average run of 200 miles a day. The boat, which he had intended to enter for the fifth Singlehanded Race, was found 300 miles west of the Canaries, floating bottom up. This is all that is known of the disappearance of her British skipper. Two explanations may be offered. He may have fallen overboard, and the boat with nobody to control her may have subsequently capsized. On the other hand, *Triple Arrow* may just as possibly have been caught in bad weather, capsized, and taken her unfortunate skipper to his death. Nor should collision with a whale be ruled out, for a few days after the trimaran was found capsized, the Italian yacht *Guia* on a racing course from Rio de Janiero to England with her crew, was sunk in twenty minutes by a large whale. The crew had time to launch a rubber liferaft and the good luck to be picked up twenty-four hours later by a Greek cargo vessel sailing for New York. This was not the first accident of this sort.

Cooke was an old hand at the Singlehanded Race since he was to come in fourth in 1972, the first British entrant home, and *Triple Arrow* would have made a formidable entrant in 1976. Fate ruled otherwise and although no firm grounds can be advanced for his disappearance, the capsizing of the trimaran swells the already lengthy list of accidents incurred by craft which, despite their speed, are certainly far more vulnerable than the traditional yacht. Indeed, *Triple Arrow* had been capsized before. She was flipped during the 1974 Round Britain Race when Cooke and his crew were bringing her into Lerwick in the Shetland Islands at the end of the third leg of the race.

Another tragedy involving a multi-hull occurred in 1968. Arthur Piver, one of the pioneers of the multi-hull and a designer who undoubtedly worked harder than anyone else to perfect them, vanished during his 500-mile qualifying cruise for the 1968 race. This American, with ever-growing experience in handling these craft, had been unable to enter in 1964 because of the delays suffered in building his boat and the consequent lack of the time he considered necessary to bring her up to racing pitch. It was on board a 33-foot trimaran that he was to put to sea for the last time.

Finally, I should like to mention the recent accident which in March 1976 so nearly cost the life of Chay Blyth while he was sailing his qualifying 500 miles. With a length of 80 feet, his trimaran, *Great Britain III* is the biggest in the world, yet she, too, capsized, after a collision with a cargo vessel filled one of her floats with water. It should, however, be added that weather conditions were bad, the wind gusting up to Force 8.

So once again the question of the stability of multi-hulls is raised. One might suppose that if in the same circumstances a mono-hull had been hit amidships, as *Great Britain III* was, she would simply have gone down. But things were not so simple as that and there is every indication that if a good mono-hull had been struck a glancing blow, as was *Great Britain III,* it would have remained upright.

One of the yachts in the 1968 race, Guy Piazzini's mono-hull ketch *Gunthur III,* twice came into collision while sailing her qualifying 500 miles in the Channel, but, despite a serious leak in the hull, she managed to make Le Havre, escorted by a fire-boat. Piazzini was able to complete repairs a few days before the start. The 1968 strikes in France had brought everything to a standstill and the dockside crane was idle, but with the help of a host of friends he successfully manhandled his yacht into the water. In the end he reached Plymouth in time, but had to retire from the race due to trouble with his rigging. This shows the difficulties faced by the singlehander in the Channel, where the volume of merchant shipping is a permanent danger to yachtsmen.

Among the entrants gathered in Millbay Dock a curious little craft painted bright yellow was tied up alongside, unnoticed save by knowing yachtsmen. Basically *Cheers* was a proa consisting simply of a couple of floats, the size and shape of very narrow canoes, built, unusually, out of cold-moulded mahogany, with the two masts stepped on one hull. One of these hulls had been fitted out in a curious way, since only one person could go below at any one time. When standing on the keel the cockpit hatch came up to your waist. Below was a sort of oval foxhole. On one side a shelf served both as galley and chart table, on the other half was the bunk. To obtain a full-length bunk the other half had to be unfolded from below the companionway which did duty as the cockpit during the day. To reduce weight to the minimum the American skipper, Tom Follett, had only taken a 5-gallon supply of drinking-water on board, which he supplemented with a few bottles of beer. A sort of hump was set on the main, or windward hull. This had been developed as a result of the capsize the boat had suffered during trials in the West Indies.

Cheers was a true proa in that she always presented the same quarter to the wind. The masts were set on the main hull. To change tacks she simply reversed direction, which was perfectly possible because there were no stays in her rigging and the whole rig could be reversed. The main hull housed a pair of centreboards one of which was lowered when the other was raised and there was also a pair of rudders operating on the same principle. Deck fittings comprised a couple of winches and a scattering of cleats. This class of craft is used by the native Malayans. *Cheers* was merely a modern version measuring 40 feet and displacing 1.34 tons. The designer, builder and part-owner was the multi-hull specialist, Dick Newick, who had entrusted her to Follett, a fifty-year-old with an uncommon personality. He had served in the US Air Force during the war, had been a merchant navy officer, practised for some years in Paris as an electronics engineer, and now operated a yacht-delivery service to the West Indies. The Singlehanded Race was to be his fourth solo crossing of the Atlantic. Those who weighed the odds before the start set him down as a potential winner when they realised that he had made the crossing singlehanded in his peculiar craft from the Virgin Islands in just over twenty-eight days. One last feature of this extraordinary vessel was that it carried no self-steering gear whatsoever. In other words, its stability had been carefully studied. In fact, *Cheers* of all the boats in the Singlehanded Race came up to Hasler's idea of the best. By reapplying ancient sailing principles Tom Follett was to steer across the ocean a craft ideally suited to singlehanded sailing. Her light displacement dictated the southerly route and this is the one which Follett was to take. As we shall see, he came very close to winning.

A multi-hull very different from *Cheers* had been entered by Bill Howell who had come in sixth in 1964 in a mono-hull. *Golden Cockerel* was a superbly fitted, exceedingly comfortable catamaran designed for cruising. She had a fairly narrow beam and her floats were extremely buoyant. In fact she was a fast and stoutly built craft, but her basic design was not ideally suited for transatlantic sailing, particularly if the weather decided to turn really nasty. She had capsized during the Crystal Trophy Race in 1967 before Howell had decided to use her for the Singlehanded Race.

Modern research on multi-hulls is only about thirty years old, very recent in fact, and there is still a great deal to be discovered about them. But one sure fact is that the lighter and faster the boat the less safe she is. The ratio between sail area and displacement makes her tricky to handle, and what is more the fact that she has no keel is of major concern in ocean racing. While to capsize a trimaran is no easy matter, it is a perfectly possible accident for a catamaran. A sudden gust of wind when the windward float is buried and the rest of the boat is insecurely balanced on the crest of a roller — and over she can go. Once she has capsized she achieves stability, and nothing can be done to right her on the spot. This is really the reason why sensible cat-men fit an escape hatch in the bottom of the boat so that they can get out if she does capsize. Such equipment was fitted to Brian Cooke's *Triple Arrow* and Alain Colas had something similar on *Pen Duick IV* for his voyage round the world. After her capsize, Howell had automatic sheet release gear fitted to *Golden Cockerel,* so that if she heeled too far all the sails would be let fly, even if the skipper was asleep below.

For many reasons multi-hulls, and particularly catamarans, are tricky boats to handle, especially if they are sailed at full stretch and on oceans liable to storm-force winds and seas. A clumsy but stoutly built mono-hull will come through really foul weather. At the worst it may be dismasted but it will keep floating like a cork. The keel will respond to pitching and rolling. A poorly designed multi-hull will behave very differently and will go over at the slightest provocation.

These risks should be taken into account at the design stage and every effort made to reduce them to the minimum. It is then up to the skipper to use his head when sailing and as his experience grows so will his sense of caution. He will have to reduce sail sooner on a multi- than on a mono-hull, however much this may go against his racing inclinations and his search for speed. These craft really can be dangerous but in their strange and efficient way they can still give that wonderful feeling of speed, with their tremendous bursts of acceleration, the long planing swooping flight which smashes the sea into a tremendous wake and produces some astonishingly high average speeds.

It was now the day before the start. The entry list had been closed since 1 May and an overall assessment could be made of the fleet which was to set sail from Plymouth. About a third of the entrants had serious prospects of winning, the remainder, and this would include over half the competitors, had gone in for the race with reasonable prospects of getting to Newport within the specified time, their boats being of much the same size as those which had already raced the course. Finally, there were a number of small boats without the slightest chance of completing the crossing in sixty days.

Each competitor was surrounded by a host of his supporters helping with the thousand-and-one last minute preparations. In Mashford's yard at the mouth of the little river which flows into the harbour, *Raph* took advantage of the last night to reset the rudder which had been removed for final checking. But it was to go on causing the skipper concern. Not far away *Sir Thomas Lipton* tugged gently at her moorings as she swung on the slight current. On board all was still. Everything was ready and Williams sat taking the air in the cockpit, giving himself one last night of peace.

To everybody's amazement, *Pen Duick IV* made her entry into Millbay Dock for the safety check after a passage of nearly 150 miles in nine hours. It was a fascinating sight. People thought they were dreaming when in came this mass of unpainted aluminium the size of a tennis court towed by a diminutive rubber dinghy with a tiny outboard engine. Unruffled, Tabarly sat at the tiller steering a trimaran so huge that it was hard to believe that one man could handle her on his own. Bill Howell reckoned the Frenchman was sailing Sydney Harbour Bridge into the dock!

The sky was overcast on the day of the start and there were occasional outbreaks of drizzle, but hardly any wind. The cliffs were thick with people and Plymouth Hoe was covered by thousands of spectators. Ferries packed to the water-line, launches of all shapes and sizes, offshore cruisers and inshore racers filled the Sound and it was hard to pick out the contestants in this mass of craft. Fortunately the wind was light. Everyone was listening for the starting gun due to be fired at 11 o'clock. The roar of wave-hopping aircraft regularly drowned the rumble of boat engines.

The race started in an almost flat calm and the competitors made feeble attempts to pass the breakwater on the tide. Four hours later *Sir Thomas Lipton* was a bare two miles from the breakwater as were *Voortrekker* and *Myth of Malham,* a fine performer in RORC races, with Noel Bevan at the helm. *Raph* and *Spirit of Cutty Sark* were closer inshore to the north while *Pen Duick* and *Cheers* had taken advantage of a slight breeze to get very slightly ahead.

Several boats were carried by the tide to the other side of the breakwater and among them Edith Baumann's 39-foot trimaran *Koala III*. She was the only woman competing and the first to have entered the Singlehanded Race. Some of them were forced to anchor, while others

90

managed to row clear of the mole. Sitting astride the bows of the centre float of his 37-foot trimaran, Commandant Waquet paddled out past the breakwater — and away to France. Stephen Pakenham, an English vicar, got out a pair of oars and quietly rowed *Rob Roy* from his native land. It was hard to imagine people like this caught in an Atlantic gale. Edith Baumann got tired of such slow progress and returned to harbour to try again a few days later. As she came into Plymouth she was surprised to come slap up against a big black 'wall' which blocked the harbour mouth and wondered on which side she should pass. Two months later she was still not one hundred per cent sure of a vessel's navigation lights, and this inexperience, which had nothing to do with her courage, was within an ace of costing her her life.

Commandant Waquet went straight back to a French port announcing that the French airline strike had forced his retirement since his navigation was to have been based upon 'fixes' radioed by planes on the transatlantic air route! Strangely enough it was under his aegis that Edith Baumann had completed her few months' novitiate in sail. The whole thing sounded completely crazy, which it might have been, but it looked far more like a publicity stunt. The Commandant was hoping to sell a whole series of trimarans which he had built and the advertising value of a crossing made by a woman would doubtless have helped nicely, even if she had gently jogged across along the trade-wind route.

For many competitors the start was a release. As Geoffrey Williams wrote in his book *Sir Thomas Lipton Wins*:

It felt as if the worried mask I had been wearing for the last nine months was swept away and I smiled despite myself. I am sure that the colour came back into my face as I realised that all the hectic preparations were over and I had won the race to Plymouth. There would be no more telephone calls, no more bills, no more well-wishers and no more crises to prevent me taking part in the race. At teatime I was happier than I had ever been and this state of mind lasted for twenty-five days.

On the day after the first night of the race news came over the wires that *Pen Duick IV* had been in collision with a cargo vessel and was being forced back to Plymouth for repairs. At midnight on the first night after the start, Tabarly had already avoided one cargo ship, when, at about three in the morning he went below to heat some coffee but a tremendous crash brought him back on deck. His windward float had hit the side of an anchored cargo ship and had scraped along its entire length as the trimaran continued under way. There was a great gash in the bows of the windward float but at the time it did not seem serious as the float comprised a series of watertight compartments and the bow compartment was packed with polystyrene foam. Everything else appeared undamaged and *Pen Duick* sailed on. However, at noon the spreaders of the mizzen snapped, threatening to bring down the whole mast and Tabarly decided to put back for repairs. He then noticed that a second compartment in the float was making water, which would in any case have forced his return.

Thanks to the flat-out work of the Royal Navy, and, needless to say, of Mashford's Yard, he was able to set out four days later in pursuit of the other boats. His hopes rose once more that nothing had been lost, although of course the boat had been tuned to nowhere near her racing pitch. Then the self-steering gear failed because it was vibrating violently at speed and *Pen Duick* had to put into Newlyn. She got away a day later only to suffer the same failure a few miles further on. This time it was the end and Tabarly had to abandon the race. At Lorient the engineers at the La Perrière yard who had built her, discovered that the collision with the cargo ship had seriously weakened the crossbeams attaching the floats to the central hull and that they would never have held for 3000 miles. It was the end of what might have proved an epic. Events four years later only went to show that Tabarly's ideas had not been so crazy after all.

The race went on and the first few days were times of constant vigilance for the competitors. 'It was impossible to sleep on Saturday night [Williams wrote], or to be out of the cockpit longer than ten minutes, because there was a great deal of shipping passing the Lizard and on two occasions I had to sail due south to avoid a collision.'

On 3 June his daily radio conversations with the shore began. At eight in the morning he announced his position, the strength and direction of the wind, the barometric pressure and the temperature. Three hours later the office of English Electric in London's Queensway gave the following information: ... 'Course 305°, change to 279° late tonight.' Trusting the computer he then altered course.

The first few days were not happy ones for all the competitors. Bruce Dalling was to break a boom, which really was rather bad luck when you remember that he had sailed 5000 miles without mishap to reach Plymouth in the first place. The crossing looked as if it was going to be a tough one, and some of the competitors found their voyage cut short when a very deep depression passed over the westbound fleet on 11 June. Marc Linski's boat *Ambrima,* a Giraglia-type yacht modified for the Singlehanded Race, was thrown on her beam ends in this storm by a freak wave. The 36-foot yacht was quite literally tossed onto her side.

It was a monster of a wave, nearly half a mile broad perhaps, and very high indeed — a real freak wave. I caught my breath in admiration and then gave way to panic pure and simple. . . I realised just

92

how helpless I was in the face of this wall of water thundering down on *Ambrima*... When the wave was barely twenty-five yards away, I dived down the cockpit as though I were diving into oblivion to escape this indescribable mass of raging sea. When the wave struck my boat I felt as if she was being pounded to pieces after having been quite literally picked up and thrown back in the water again.

Although the wave had done an impressive amount of damage, the rigging had held. However, the rudder had been torn off and what was worse Linski realised after twenty minutes that the boat was making water fast. A crack over 6 feet long had been forced open at the point where the keel was fixed to the hull. It was not a gaping crack, or else the yacht would have sunk like a stone, but it was bad enough for the water to seep in. The race was over as far as *Ambrima* was concerned and the question now was whether her skipper would come out of it alive. The first thing to be done was to rig a jury rudder and to make for home. Spain was 1200 miles away. An exhausting struggle began as Linski divided his time between working the boat and manning the pump to control the leak which he had plugged with tallow and white lead, first nailing a piece of canvas and then a plank over it. He had no radio transmitter on which to send out distress signals. For eight days the stricken yacht limped along until Linski was 90 miles from the coast, where a Spanish fishing-boat picked her up and passed her a tow. Linski was safe, but five hours later, on 21 June, his boat foundered. The next morning Linski found himself in Corcubion a little fishing harbour near La Coruña. Two days' rest and home he went to Marseilles. He was to return for the 1972 Singlehanded Race, in a bigger and certainly sturdier boat, but with the same lust for life.

The trimaran which Joan de Kat had built was to disintegrate and sink on the same longitude as Linski's boat but a little further to the north. At the end of his first singlehanded crossing by the trade wind route in 1964, de Kat had reached Newport at the close of the second Singlehanded Race, met such competitors as Chichester and Tabarly, and determined to enter for the third race. He threw himself into the design of an ultra-light trimaran to be built of 9 mm marine plywood, presented the plans to the Fondation de la Vocation in 1965 and obtained a grant which enabled him to lay her down. For three years de Kat was to devote himself to winning the Singlehanded Race. He is a charming and friendly person, but he was to treat the sea too lightly.

Right from the start his homemade craft was to cause him concern. The key elements only held together by a miracle and at first he thought of retiring or at least of putting back because of a serious rigging defect which made him rightly fear for the safety of his mast. His navigation, too, was slightly out for when dawn broke there was the Casquets Light,

1. A few minutes before the start, with *Raph* in the foreground an the sails of *Pen Duick IV* outlined against the old-fashioned gaf rig of a Thames barge.

2. Bruce Dalling's *Voortrekker*, which so very nearly won.

3. Eric Tabarly working on the faulty self-steering gear which wa to force him to abandon the race.

4. *Cheers*, the strange proa which could only catch the wind on th same quarter.

5. The American, Tom Follett, whose performance on the souther route was to amaze all competitors.

6. Interior of *Cheers*. Follett was to spend 27 days in this foxho with all his provisions and gear.

7. *Myth of Malham* skippered by Noel Bevan and so well-known RORC circles. She was to meet a sad fate when she foundered the Channel.

8. Bill Howell's catamaran *Golden Cockerel*.

9. Marc Linski aboard *Ambrima*. When she sank in the Nor Atlantic, he was picked up by a Spanish trawler.

10. Stephen Pakenham rowing *Rob Roy* out of Plymouth harbour the start.

11. Edith Baumann and *Koala III*. The trimaran sank north of th Azores and her skipper returned to Brest on board a warship.

12. Joan de Kat's trimaran *Yaksha*. She went down to the west Ireland but her skipper was brought safely ashore.

13. Commandant Waquet goes home—to France—paddling all tl way!

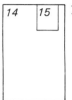

14. *Sir Thomas Lipton* and her skipper Geoffrey Williams (15) wl owed his victory to strict planning—and a little luck!

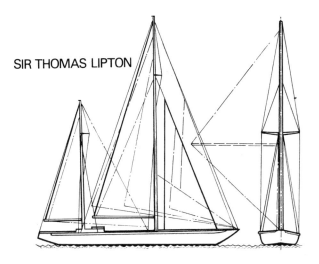

SIR THOMAS LIPTON

1968—Geoffrey Williams—*Sir Thomas Lipton*—25 days 20 hrs 33 mins

> Length: 56 feet (mono-hull)
> GRP sandwich hull
> Ketch-rigged
> Architect: Robert Clark
> Builder: Derek Kelsall (England)

which guards the Channel Isles, instead of Plymouth to which he thought he was heading! He finished up in Braye Harbour in Alderney for repairs and the welcome feel of land under his feet. At one time he thought of giving up, but finally set sail and only passed Plymouth once more on 6 June on course for America.

The mast collar which he had had to repair in Alderney soon caused renewed concern. Since the shrouds were attached to it, it was an absolutely vital part of the rigging. When it threatened to part completely, de Kat was momentarily discouraged and thought of putting into an Irish port. Then he decided to effect repairs himself by using the lower collar, which was about to give way, to reinforce the upper collar which still seemed to be holding good and which supported the shrouds for the floats. Later the self-steering gear went wrong, but de Kat managed to repair it by daylight. These repairs were not effective for very long.

Next, the central hull began to make water so fast aft that he had to bail out with a bucket. Finally the aft crossbeam securing the central hull to the port float started to show signs of weakness and then snapped so that the only attachment was the forward beam. Once again de Kat managed to effect jury repairs before nightfall. Early the next morning he discovered that the port float had vanished. He now had to act quickly, for if the boat rolled to port, there was nothing to stop her turning right over and floating bottom up. De Kat cut through the shrouds one by one so as to reduce the height of his mast. He then flew to his radio transmitter, tuned in to the emergency frequency and began to send out distress signals, giving his position. By a lucky chance a Scandinavian airliner picked up his call. He then inflated and launched his rubber dinghy.

I tried to keep calm. I had plenty of time to choose what I would need for ten days' drifting around on the ocean — food, biscuits, tinned food (not forgetting the tin-opener) and 5 gallons of drinking water; then my sleeping-bag (even if it got wet it would keep me from the cold) . . . my chronometer, my little transistor in its bag, the rockets in their waterproof wrappings, my torch, my storm lantern which could provide me with a little heat, matches . . . then one last radio call, telling the world that I was abandoning the trimaran. The answer comes: 'Good luck!'

The starboard float then went and *Yaksha* had little longer to live. The liferaft drifted away on the angry seas, rising on the waves and sinking into valleys formed by the rollers. Sometimes there would be a thunderous roar and de Kat would ride for 20 yards on the surf of a breaking wave. This was to last for sixty hours before de Kat picked up messages about him on his transistor, and knew a rescue operation had been mounted. An aircraft came over and he sent up some rockets, but they were not spotted. At last, on 20 June, an RAF Shackleton sighted the rockets sent up by the liferaft. It dropped a rescue dinghy with survival packs by parachute and directed the Norwegian bulk-carrier, *Jagona,* to pick him up. So de Kat found himself heading for Russia on board *Jagona* instead of for America on board his peculiar three-hulled craft *Yaksha.*

Edith Baumann chose the southern route which passes slightly to the north of the Azores. As stated she delayed her departure because of lack of wind. Her boat, *Koala III,* was a 39-foot trimaran with comfortable living-quarters in the large central hull, to which the floats were attached by the crossbeams which were to be the reason for the yacht's retirement. Following five continuous days' bad weather, one of the floats looked as if it was going to come adrift. The forward beam had snapped and the side-strut supporting the centre beam was torn away. Gradually the float worked more and more loose and then one after the other the aft port beam and the forward starboard beam snapped. *Koala III* was roughly 150 miles to the north of the Azores and unable to head for the islands under sail. In the afternoon Edith sent out a distress signal, giving her approximate position and calling all ships. There was no answer. Next she sighted a cargo vessel which kept on its course not realising that the trimaran was in difficulties. Next morning the boat was still safely afloat and Edith was able to contact Radio Saint-Lys and speak directly with Commandant Waquet. She described her situation, with the trimaran crippled but still standing up to the heavy seas. Waquet then set the rescue operation in motion and ordered Edith to stand by to launch her dinghy should the trimaran start to break up. In the end she was spotted by an American Air Force Hercules which directed the German vessel *Magdalena Vinnen* to the scene, but the sea was so rough that she could not get near the yacht. An aircraft took off from the American base at Terceira in the Azores and dropped luminous marker buoys round *Koala III* as well as a radio marker buoy to help rescuers. In the end the *Henri Poincaré* put a dinghy alongside the trimaran and picked up Edith, still clutching her dog. She was then transferred by lifeboat to another French ship, the *Guépratte,* which brought her back to Brest.

This was the third serious accident and but for the rescue services it might have ended in tragedy. People talk about Edith's bravery, and while she certainly had plenty of courage, what else could she do if the boat really were breaking up under her? She simply had to face up to the situation. She had plenty of time to get ready to abandon ship and to organise her own rescue from the shelter of the main hull. The only thing for which she could be blamed was for going to sea in a boat which was not built for an Atlantic crossing, but how was she able to predict how it would behave in heavy seas, given that her experience of sailing was, to all intents and purposes, non-existent? Whatever Commandant Waquet may say, you can't make a sailor in six months, much less one who has to race a non-stop course of 3000 miles singlehanded. Some storms are too much for the most skilled seamen and the stoutest boats.

These mishaps served to strengthen the safety regulations enforced in subsequent races and to harden the hearts of the Race Committee against such whimsical craft as they had allowed to start in 1968. Judging one's own competence to enter was no longer enough.

Ten days after the start, and after seventeen of the twenty-eight boats remaining in the race had given their positions, a pattern of the leading yachts began to emerge. Three of the fleet were fighting for the lead: the British yacht *Sir Thomas Lipton,* the South African *Voortrekker* and the French *Raph. Spirit of Cutty Sark* was some hundred miles behind

101

the leaders and with 800 miles of the race sailed they were 150 miles ahead of the position reached by Eric Tabarly at the same stage of his victory in 1964.

Now that *Pen Duick IV* had retired, four mono-hulls made up the five favourites — the fifth being Bill Howell's *Golden Cockerel*. There was no news of *Cheers* which had taken a very southerly route and, apart from the leaders, it was hard to obtain a true picture of the state of the race since the competitors had taken a wide variety of routes and were not always able to report their positions.

Meanwhile an unruffled Geoffrey Williams was sailing along the Great Circle route, correcting his course each day in the light of the information given to him by the computer. When the long-range forecast indicated a track away from the Great Circle route, he would bear it in mind when making his final choice. In order to feed valid information into the computer, *Sir Thomas Lipton* had been fitted with a complete range of instruments to record the wind-strength, the speed and position of the boat, and numerous other factors. To report his position, Williams needed a very powerful transmitter, electric wiring, aerials, batteries and generating engine. Without making too much of all this gadgetry, it is interesting to see how programming the route was undertaken.

First, at about 5.30 each morning, a computer situated outside London would make up a forecast map for the next forty-eight hours which would go to English Electric's Queensway office. There it would be fed into another computer. Williams would radio his position to David Thorpe of the *The Daily Telegraph* at eight o'clock and this would be passed on to Queensway. From the course and speed of *Sir Thomas Lipton* her position at 11 am was predicted and fed into the computer to be co-ordinated with the weather map.

All the courses available to *Sir Thomas Lipton* were then projected as a fan on the grid of the forecast map. The computer stored the data on the boat's performance in the form of polar curves. At each intersection of the yacht's possible course and the intersection of a value of wind speed and direction, it would calculate the speed of the boat.

This operation changed the fan into a series of speeds. The bearings of the three best tracks were then radioed to *Sir Thomas Lipton* at 11 am. It was then up to the skipper to select the best track.

Over and above this highly scientific organisation of the navigation, intelligent research had also been applied to the problems of simplifying the handling of the foresails. *Sir Thomas Lipton* was rigged with several forestays to which the jibs were permanently bent. They were kept on deck in long, laced-up covers, an arrangement which avoided the need to stow these particularly heavy and cumbersome sails below deck. As Chichester had done in 1964, so Williams spared himself the dangers of handling a spinnaker in a following wind by having a pair of running sails with booms set high up on the mast.

The tenth of June was to be the crucial day of the whole race. The long-range weather forecasts were to pay off and *Sir Thomas Lipton* was successfully to pass to the north of the deep depression which was to cause so much trouble to the other boats. Although he was in fact a mere 50 miles to the north of *Voortrekker,* this was enough to escape the worst of the gale. The South African suffered appalling weather conditions which slowed him down considerably; *Raph* also took some heavy punishment and the bad weather was to be one of the causes of the failure of her self-steering gear; the Frenchman André Foezon's sloop *Sylvia II* was dismasted and forced to return to Plymouth, though she put to sea again and eventually finished twelfth; while *Golden Cockerel* rode out the assault of the gigantic waves and storm force winds under bare poles. After the race, Bill Howell was to admit with a cheerfulness which did not completely cover his concern, that he had seldom been so frightened in his life and that he would never again sail a catamaran in the North Atlantic. (All the same, in 1972 and 1976, he was at the start once again in the same catamaran, renamed *Tahiti Bill,* though he was forced to retire after colliding with a Russian trawler only a few miles from the finish.)

Gliksman in *Raph* had to put in to Newfoundland to repair his self-steering gear. Three weeks after the start, and when he was right up with Williams, the rudder-tab actuated by the wind-vane had been wrenched off. Help was organised in St John's and a few days later the part reached its destination. The gear was repaired and *Raph* put to sea again. Fresh trouble then forced Gliksman into Saint-Pierre-et-Miquelon and the race was over as far as he was concerned.

I could have made repairs at Saint-Pierre-et-Miquelon [he was to write later] and finished the race. I was less than a week away from Newport, the ice and bad weather were behind me now. Once the Grand Banks are left astern the sun scatters the fog and every day takes you a little further south ... I kept thinking that the whole fleet was poised to enter Newport, and I could not bear the idea of coming into a half-full yacht basin and my shoulders shrank merely to imagine the sympathy, however sincere, which would greet me.

It was a tremendous disappointment for Gliksman, but a great experience to have taken the lead in a mono-hull like *Raph.* (Four years later he was to reach Newport aboard a quite outstanding little boat in a time which no other competitor could match.)

The last two-thirds of the race were remarkable for their very light winds, and *Sir Thomas Lipton* had to make forty-two changes of course in a single day to catch the winds which would keep her on the right heading. On another day Williams spent ten hours at a stretch constantly changing sails and steering by hand, without a moment's rest. For eighteen solid hours he ran before a 9-knot breeze under more than 3000 sq feet of canvas. It took him three days to clear the iceberg zone and for most of that time he could not even see his bows. Having weighed up the situation, he came to the conclusion that an intermittent watch was no better than no watch at all, and so he dragged his liferaft into the cockpit and put three weeks' provisions on board. Then he retired to the cabin. So, with nobody on lookout, *Sir Thomas Lipton* charged along, sometimes hitting 10 knots, through an area in which four icebergs had been reported.

Much further away to the south Tom Follett's strange craft was eating up the miles and heading swiftly for her goal. Although he had chosen the longer route he had sunshine and following winds all the way. By the finish he had only had to make a dozen tacks in the entire crossing! There was an even more surprising sequel: *Cheers* registered 384 fewer miles on her log than *Sir Thomas Lipton*. This means that when you take into account the constant beating which those who follow the Great Circle route encounter, Tom Follett sailed fewer miles through the water. But you need as fantastic a craft as *Cheers* to be lying second the day before you come in, after having selected the southerly route. Of all the competitors Follett achieved the best run in twenty-four hours — 225 nautical miles as compared with *Sir Thomas Lipton*'s best run of 211 miles.

Earlier, I devoted considerable space to the discussion of routes, so that the options taken by the different competitors could be properly understood. In fact the distance run by *Sir Thomas Lipton* was 3784 miles, *Voortrekker* ran 3750 and *Cheers* just 3400. So we see that in 1968 it was still possible for a boat specially designed to run before the wind to take the southerly route and beat by a whisker a mono-hull which had taken the Great Circle. Nowadays this is far harder in view of the advances made in improving the sailing qualities of multi-hulls hard on the wind.

Sir Thomas Lipton was approaching Nantucket. A jammed mizzen halyard had taken her northwards of her intended course, but eventually Williams managed to climb the mast and cut the halyard. He then decided to look at his sailing instructions where he noticed that nowhere was it laid down that he had to pass south of the Nantucket Light Vessel. His instructions simply said 'south of Nantucket', and he therefore decided, after consulting the chairman of the race committee, Lieutenant-Colonel Odling-Smee on the radio, that he would pass 14 miles to the north of the Nantucket Light and south of Nantucket Island itself. In fact it appears that at the briefing before the start of the race competitors were instructed to pass to the south of the Light Vessel but that no written amendment was made to their sailing instructions. Williams was not at the briefing, so he went by the letter of the law. Lack of precision on this point in the rules of the 1968 race was corrected in the sailing instructions for 1972, in which the Light Vessel was mentioned, but in 1976 the yachts were not required to leave the Vessel to starboard. For 1980 it is again a mark for the course.

Twenty-five days after the start Williams observed a flash from Cape Buzzard Lighthouse, only five degrees to starboard of its estimated position on the chart, although he had been unable to take a sun-sight for three weeks. A few hours later he was crossing the finishing-line as winner.

Tearfully, I passed the Tower at 7.30 GMT. We rode on together for a few minutes and then I went forward and dropped all the sails into untidy heaps on the deck. For a while, losing the sails seemed to make no difference; but slowly the log started to fall, and after an age *Lipton* was still. Still for the first time in three and a half weeks. Now it was all over and I was completely satisfied.

The twelve hour penalty imposed on Williams at the start had run out when *Voortrekker* was sighted off Nantucket, but she did not cross the finishing line until seventeen hours after *Sir Thomas Lipton*. Bruce Dalling appeared very drawn from his voyage and exhausted from lack of sleep. As far as he was concerned the race started badly when his boom broke away from the mast and carried the mainsail overboard. After a sustained and hard struggle he had managed to recover them both, but on several occasions he was forced to repair his self-steering gear which showed signs of weakness, and some of his winches gave up the ghost. But for the storm of mid-June, he might well have made Newport ahead of Williams. This delightful athlete took a very good second place on a boat which may have been hard to handle but which was perfectly fitted for the sort of race she sailed. Thus two big ketches took the honours, and but for mechanical trouble there is every reason to believe that *Raph* would have been up with the winners. The soundness of the thinking behind the light hull and divided rigging design was amply vindicated. Once again it was a victory for boats with powerful sailing qualities to windward, crewed by real technicians of ocean racing. The first two men in on elapsed time had devoted a great deal of thought to the design of their boats, made a close study of the weather conditions likely to be encountered during the race, and had gone into strict training for the event like real athletes. Drop-outs, dreamers and ocean wanderers no longer had any business to be in the race. Or to be more accurate had little chance of coming in among the winners if they did enter. If you discount the obviously modest remarks of the first men home to Newport, you will find that not one of them regards singlehanded sailing as anything but the serious business which it has become.

Once again the multi-hulls had to play second fiddle to the big and efficient mono-hulls. Nevertheless, *Cheers* came in only eleven hours behind the second boat and very nearly upset everyone's predictions. She was, in fact, a very special sort of multi-hull and Tom Follett handled her in a way that was all his own. His race will go down in the history of the Singlehanded Race, for with the minimum of special gear and a great deal of sound sense he very nearly put paid to two perfectly equipped craft, with their electronic gadgets and their self-steering gear. His magnificent achievement was utterly in the original spirit of the race, and his remarkable third place was justly admired. In 1972, Tom Follett was to enter *Three Cheers,* a triple-hull this time, and was closely watched by all the experts.

Leslie Williams took fourth place with his big *Spirit of Cutty Sark* and the sheer strength of his own two hands. Her huge sail area gave the skipper a great deal of trouble and it was very hard to get the maximum sailing efficiency out of his boat. With large headsails like hers, it was impossible to carry a setting absolutely suited to the weather of the moment, since the skipper had always to be looking ahead and an-ticipating conditions so as not to be caught over-canvassed. His fourth place was, therefore, all the more well deserved.

A closer contest had been expected between the mono- and the multi-hulls. The first catamaran home, *Golden Cockerel,* only finished in fifth place and although she had always been up among the leaders, she could not really make her mark because of the bad weather which she encountered on the Great Circle route. The retirement of *Pen Duick IV* was bound to upset the odds in any battle between mono- and multi-hulls. She was the only boat which could have given the winner a fight if only there had been time to prepare her properly. This was precisely the thing on which Williams based his victory. A trimaran of such size and revolutionary design could only be dangerous in so far as the weak points which were bound to exist in her had been revealed and remedied in pre-race trials.

Brian Cooke's *Opus* provided a shock sixth place, since she was a typical cruising yacht with no concessions made to ocean racing. Only an extraordinary personal performance by her skipper could have given her this achievement.

Gancia Girl (ex-*Toria*) was the first trimaran to be placed. She came in ahead of Illingworth's famous cutter *Myth of Malham.* Among the 18 boats placed, the tenth, a production boat called *Maguelonne,* entered by the Frenchman, Jean-Yves Terlain, should not be overlooked. He regarded this race as a reconnaissance in strength for the next contest, which he was to sail four years later as the favourite on a vast 128-foot, three-masted schooner.

There was a notable list of retirements. Apart from the comedians who belonged there in any case, the particularly bad weather caused severe damage to a number of serious entrants, and 1968 marks an important turning point in the history of the Singlehanded Race. It gained the reputation of a contest which was not to be taken lightly, although this did not stop the numbers of entrants from increasing every time it was held. Only a handful of enthusiasts took the classification on handicap seriously, and in any case the rules were not framed to enhance its importance. Choosing the biggest manageable boat and skippering it singlehanded is considered to carry the greatest cachet. As we shall see, a different system was adopted for the next race and these rules were still further revised for 1976. Handicapping is exceedingly difficult in a race as long as the Singlehanded as the constant changes introduced from 1960 onwards go to show. The real object of the exercise is to get to Newport first. The fairest solution was to create a number of different events within the overall scope of the race and have separate classes for each of them, and that is what the race committee decided for the 1976 and 1980 events.

RESULTS OF THE 1968 SINGLEHANDED RACE

START: 1 JUNE

1	GEOFFREY WILLIAMS (GB)	*Sir Thomas Lipton*
	Ketch: 56 feet	25 days 20 hrs 33 mins
2	BRUCE DALLING (S Africa)	*Voortrekker*
	Ketch: 49 feet	26 days 13 hrs 42 mins
3	TOM FOLLETT (USA)	*Cheers*
	Proa: 40 feet	27 days 00 hrs 13 mins
4	LESLIE WILLIAMS (GB)	*Spirit of Cutty Sark*
	Sloop: 53 feet	29 days 10 hrs 17 mins
5	BILL HOWELL (Aus)	*Golden Cockerel*
	Catamaran (ketch): 43 feet	31 days 16 hrs 24 mins
6	BRIAN COOKE (GB)	*Opus*
	Sloop: 32 feet	34 days 08 hrs 23 mins
7	M. J. MINTER-KEMP (GB)	*Gancia Girl*
	Trimaran (ketch): 42 feet	34 days 13 hrs 15 mins
8	NOEL BEVAN (GB)	*Myth of Malham*
	Cutter: 39 feet	36 days 01 hrs 41 mins

9	B. DE CASTELBAJAC (France)	*Maxine*
	Sloop: 34 feet	37 days 13 hrs 47 mins
10	JEAN-YVES TERLAIN (France)	*Magnelonne*
	Sloop: 34 feet	38 days 09 hrs 10 mins
11	NIGEL BURGESS (GB)	*Dogwatch*
	Sloop: 27 feet	38 days 12 hrs 13 mins
12	ANDRÉ FOEZON (France)	*Silvia II**
	Sloop: 35 feet	40 days 00 hrs 16 mins
13	B. ENBOM (Sweden)	*Fione*
	Sloop: 19 feet	40 days 10 hrs 13 mins
14	CLAUS HEHNER (W Germany)	*Mex*
	Sloop: 37 feet	41 days 12 hrs 46 mins
15	REV STEPHEN PAKENHAM (GB)	*Rob Roy*
	Ketch: 32 feet	42 days 03 hrs 49 mins
16	COLIN FORBES (GB)	*Startled Faun*
	Trimaran: 33 feet	45 days 10 hrs 08 mins
17	BERNIE RODRIGUEZ (USA)	*Amistad*
	Trimaran: 25 feet	47 days 18 hrs 05 mins
18	MICHAEL RICHEY (GB)	*Jester*
	Sloop: 25 feet	57 days 10 hrs 40 mins
19	E. MATTSON (Sweden)	*Goodwin II*
	Sloop: 19 feet	disqualified

Retirements

ERIC WILLIS (GB)	*Coila*
Trimaran (ketch): 50 feet	1 July: drinking water contaminated 300 miles from Newport
ERIC TABARLY (France)	*Pen Duick IV*
Trimaran (ketch): 67 feet	2 June: collision
W. WALLIN (Sweden)	*Wileca*
Sloop: 26 feet	6 June: too cold
A. CAROZZO (Italy)	*San Giorgio*
Catamaran (ketch): 54 feet	27 June: rudder trouble
B. WAQUET (France)	*Tamouré*
Trimaran: 37 feet	1 June: went straight home, 'French airlines on strike'
D. PILE (GB)	*Atlantis III*
Ketch: 25 feet	19 June: trouble with self-steering gear

*Restarted 19 June: elapsed time 29 days, 16 minutes

108

MISS E. BAUMANN (W Germany)
Trimaran: 39 feet
Koala III
26 June: abandoned
ship off the Azores

M. J. PULSFORD (GB)
Trimaran: 30 feet
White Ghost
4 July: rudder trouble

S. MUNRO (GB)
Catamaran: 45 feet
Ocean Highlander
4 June: dismasted

L. PAILLARD (France)
Sloop: 30 feet
La Délirante
23 June: broken mast

A. GLIKSMAN (France)
Yawl: 57 feet
Raph
21 June: rudder trouble

J. DE KAT (France)
Trimaran: 49 feet
Yaksha
18 June: broke up and
sank

M. CUIKLINSKI (France)
Sloop: 35 feet
Ambrima
12 June: hull severely
damaged, dismasted
and sank under tow

R. G. M. WINGATE (GB)
Sloop: 39 feet
Zeevalk
19 June: trouble with
self-steering gear

F. HEINEMANN (W Germany)
Sloop: 33 feet
Aye-Aye
30 June: trouble with
self-steering gear

G. PIAZZINI (Switzerland)
Ketch: 41 feet
Gunthur III
13 June: trouble with
mast-step

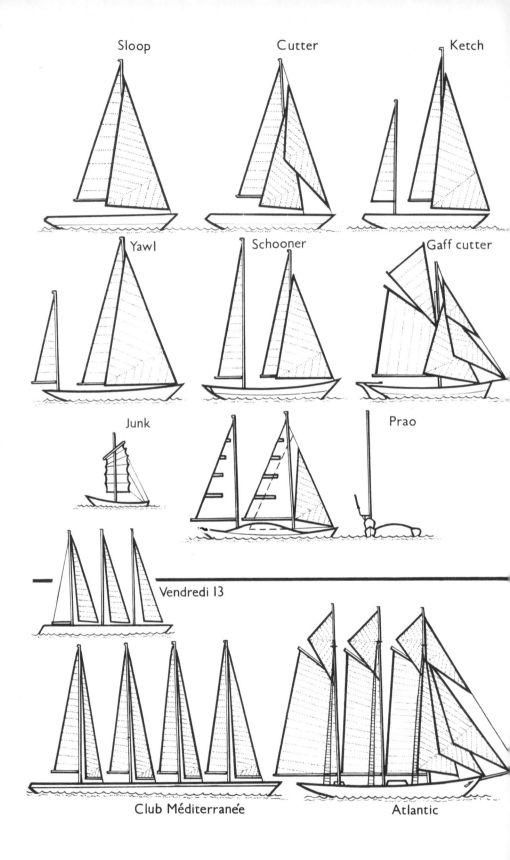

Sloop
Cutter
Ketch
Yawl
Schooner
Gaff cutter
Junk
Prao
Vendredi 13
Club Méditerranée
Atlantic

CHAPTER SIX

The First Multi-hull Winner

The 1972 race beat plenty of records even before the starting gun boomed at Plymouth. The number of entrants was impressive, with fifty-five boats let loose upon the Atlantic. As far as size was concerned, *Vendredi 13* led the field with her 128 feet in exaggerated contrast to the 19 feet of *Willing Griffin*. There was a high proportion of multi-hulls, the best of which were to take the direct route and try to beat the mono-hulls on their own ground. But the big question was whether the gigantic three-master would succeed in dominating the field.

There had been few changes in the rules for this fourth race, but a number of precise revisions had been made. This time all entrants were obliged to complete their 500 qualifying miles before 17 April. That is, two months before the start. And this time each boat had to have completed 500 miles of solo sailing, too, though not necessarily with the entrant at the helm. As before, engines were permitted, but only to provide power for the yacht's instruments and navigation lights, but not to assist sail-handling or weighing anchor. Nor could they be used to assist the self-steering gear, although in fact in 1972 for the first time the Committee allowed the use of electrical self-steering gear provided the energy was self-generated. The gear had to be fed from a battery separate from the main batteries and charged by a wind-vane, a water-impeller activated by the speed of the boat, or by solar panels. Thus the self-steering gear had more or less to be powered from a source exclusive to itself. Using electricity to drive the gear is important because it means the gear can be that much stronger and so much more suitable for boats with a larger displacement. Electrically-driven gear maintains a constant course, which is of some advantage when sailing close inshore or in dangerous conditions. If the wind changes direction the sails will require to be reset and the boat will be held up if the single-hander is unaware of what has happened. Self-steering gear controlled by a vane cannot keep the boat on course when the wind changes, but it does have the advantage of keeping the sails permanently adjusted. In these circumstances it is a good thing to have it fitted with an alarm

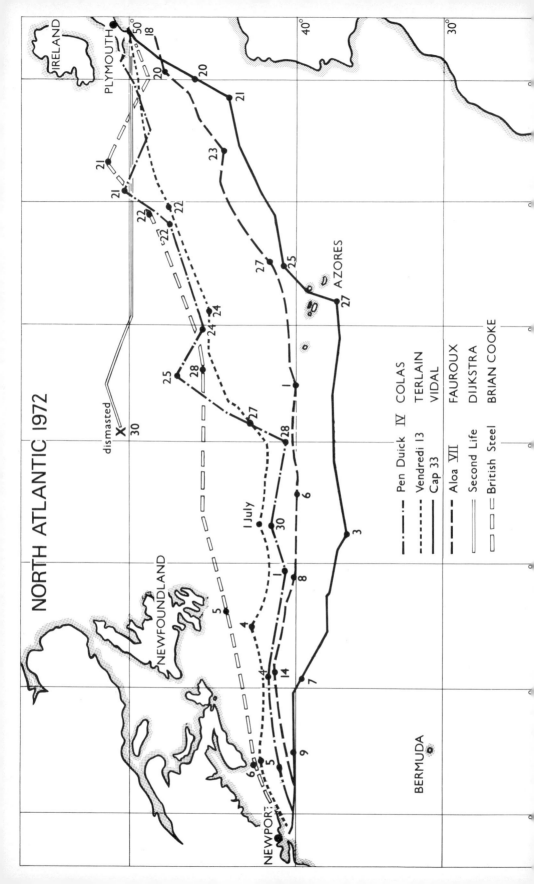

NORTH ATLANTIC 1972

IRELAND

PLYMOUTH

50°

18

20

20

21

23

21

21

22

22

22

27

25

AZORES

27

24

24

25

28

24

27

28

dismasted

30

1 July

28

6

30

3

1

8

NEWFOUNDLAND

5

4

5

14

7

BERMUDA

6

5

9

NEWPORT

40°

30°

Pen Duick IV COLAS
Vendredi 13 TERLAIN
Cap 33 VIDAL
Aloa VII FAUROUX
Second Life DIJKSTRA
British Steel BRIAN COOKE

system which goes off when the boat wanders from her course.

From 1968 onwards several single-handers had used this equipment, but in 1972 virtually all the boats were still fitted either with Hasler or Atom gear or with one of their own invention, which some entrants had supplemented with electric self-steering.

As far as radio was concerned, a few boats were fitted with single sideband sets, and provided they were maintained in working order they had a very wide range, easily covering the entire North Atlantic. Others had medium-wave receiver-transmitters. Although their range was only about 300 miles, they could be used for ship-to-ship conversations. It should not be forgotten that during the race boats were not allowed to receive outside assistance nor could they be escorted. On the other hand they could put into harbour and were allowed to be towed for up to 2 miles, provided that this was not in the direction of the finish. Thus they were allowed to take on supplies and equipment and to make repairs, but only in part.

This was a perfectly sensible rule since any boat taking advantage of it more or less forfeited any chance of winning, given the performance of the other entrants who had had no breakdowns, because of the time lost. It was a rule that was to play a vital part in the 1976 race.

Receivers for weather facsimile maps were allowed, and Alain Colas was to have one fitted to *Pen Duick IV,* but on the other hand radar, and hyperbolic navigational aids such as Decca and Loran were banned, as were prearranged signals for individual competitors. Thus the system which Williams had perfected for 1968 was outlawed.

The Observer Trophy was still awarded to the winner on elapsed time, but there were also three other trophies, offered for the winners on handicap in each of the mono-hull and multi-hull classes and the first boat home under 35 feet overall. The handicap which a Royal Western Yacht Club committee had worked out in days, hours and minutes was based upon the largest boat entered, in this case *Vendredi 13,* which was regarded as the scratch-boat. Every other boat in the fleet was given an allowance of the number of days and hours the committee expected that boat to be behind *Vendredi 13* if she were sailed well.

Finally it should be noted that the sailing instructions prescribed that whatever route chosen from Plymouth to Newport, the Nantucket Light Vessel should be passed to starboard.

If single-handed ocean racing had been in its infancy in 1960, things were very different in 1972. Since the third race in 1968 a number of important events had occurred in the history of single-handed ocean sailing. Tabarly had won the Transpacific Singlehanded Race in thirty-nine days, fifteen hours, forty-four minutes in *Pen Duick V.* Five boats had entered for the event, which was twice the distance of the transatlantic and Jean-Yves Terlain had come in second in *Blue Arpège.* While

Terlain was to start as favourite in the 1972 Singlehanded Race, Tabarly did not enter. As we shall see, he had sold his trimaran to Alain Colas, and in July 1972 was back in the Pacific with his crew to repeat his victory in *Pen Duick III* in the fully crewed Los Angeles-Tahiti Race.

On the other hand Sir Francis Chichester had entered in his latest boat *Gipsy Moth V*. The performance of her predecessor, in which he had made his circumnavigation of the globe with only one stop at Sydney, had not completely satisfied him and he had had a ketch 57 feet long built to Robert Clark's design. In this boat, before June 1972, he had set up a record by sailing singlehanded 4000 miles in twenty-two days in the Atlantic trade winds. He was not entirely pleased with this since he had aimed to complete the distance in twenty days, that is, at 200 miles a day. None the less, it must be said that an average daily run of 181 miles is still pretty good for the singlehander. And Chichester was seventy-one at the time!

Although it might not have had any direct influence upon the Transatlantic Race, *The Sunday Times* singlehanded race round the world which started in the summer of 1968 marks an important stage in the history of singlehanded racing. It was won by Robin Knox-Johnston in three hundred and thirteen days non-stop in *Suhali,* a seaworthy boat, of course, but heavy and rather slow all the same. The race was organised by *The Sunday Times* and was to give rise to various unexpected occurrences, among them the strange story of Donald Crowhurst, who sent messages indicating he was in the lead, but in fact never left the Atlantic and then disappeared, and the retirement of Bernard Moitessier, who was in the lead when he headed away to Tahiti. He was to sail non-stop and singlehanded more than one and a half times round the world.

No history of singlehanded sailing would be complete without mentioning Chay Blyth who, in 1971, accomplished the feat of sailing round the world south of the three southern capes in an east-west direction, that is, against the prevailing winds. His 59-foot ketch, *British Steel,* was also designed by Robert Clark. He was to complete his circumnavigation in three hundred and two days, a feat never achieved by any other man. Although Blyth himself did not enter the 1972 race, his boat was there, skippered by Brian Cooke.

By contrast with these marathon races round the world, the Singlehanded Race is a sprint event. Of course everything is relative, but the winner of this fifth race in the series would have to be extremely hard-headed. The first three places in 1968 had been so close that there was every indication that the competition would be even more merciless this time. Of the fifty-nine boats entered, fifty-five actually started and forty were placed. Of the other twelve, three took more than sixty days to reach Newport, and the rest retired for various reasons.

This testing race had attracted plenty of French competitors and some pretty formidable boats were at the start. *Vendredi 13*, skippered by Jean-Yves Terlain, undoubtedly attracted the most attention, representing as she did an entirely new approach to singlehanded sailing. Although Terlain had never won yet, he had nevertheless taken part in a 3000-mile Transatlantic and a 6000-mile Transpacific Race. Over a long period he had had time to go very deeply into the singlehander's problems. He had then had the amazing notion of designing a very long boat, very simply rigged with three jib sails. The American naval architect, Dick Carter, had recently become known in Europe for the originality of his designs. Terlain discussed matters with him in New York and managed to win him over to use his ruthless logic to design the boat. This logic was based on the premise that the speed of a yacht is proportionate to her length on the water-line. By making the schooner slim, ultra-light and setting one, two or three sails according to weather conditions — relatively easy to handle because the sails were boomed jibs, Carter reasoned that *Vendredi 13* ought to walk away from the opposition in the stiff westerlies which prevail in the North Atlantic. The other side of the picture was as obvious — that a boat carrying so little canvas would be unhandy in light winds and unable to achieve her full potential when sailing with the wind, while her very size meant that every single piece of equipment had to be of the highest quality, for the slightest failure was potentially disastrous. From the start of her sea-going trials, it was soon apparent that she was a one-trim boat — for sailing hard on the wind. To make good her lack of canvas in light winds, three vast genoas were prepared and laid ready on deck for setting. They could only be raised in very light winds — in fact Terlain was to use them hardly at all — since the boat had been hastily rigged and in particular the sheaves at the mastheads had not been designed to carry such a large sail area as the genoas. Nevertheless, the length of the boat would give her that extra horsepower in the stiff winds and strong Atlantic swells, and the ease with which Terlain handled his giant singlehanded made people think he would be hard to beat.

Despite the vast scale of the operation everything worked out according to plan. Had there been a little more time and a greater degree of co-ordination, it would have been possible to improve still further the boat's sailing potential. Had she been lighter and stouter, with sheet tracks to stop the sails pulling out of shape, her speed would undoubtedly have been improved. It is easy to be wise after the event, but when you know just how much it takes to bring an ordinary yacht up to racing pitch, you realise the difficulties which Terlain and his helpers had to meet and to overcome. It should be remembered that this was the very first yacht of its kind to be built in a boatyard and if it was possible to find theoretically satisfying solutions to the plans, it was a very different matter when it came to giving them practical application.

In an operation on this scale, money soon came to the forefront and after lengthy discussions and soaking him in all the wonderful, traditional atmosphere of Cowes Week Terlain was able to convince the French film magnate, Claude Lelouch, of the soundness of his schemes. Without Lelouch the boat would undoubtedly never have seen the light of day and this seems the appropriate point to congratulate him on his sporting spirit and his boldness, even if the yacht was subsequently to become the star of a film. The design and construction of a boat like her takes an extravagant sum of money and a contract between the film man and the graduate of the Ecole des Beaux Arts was duly signed and sealed, Jean-Yves Terlain undertaking subsequently to repay Lelouch a proportion of the monies which had been advanced.

The self-steering gear on *Vendredi 13* was of the same type fitted to engine-driven vessels. An electric motor controlled magnetically by the compass acted upon the rudder. The system could be linked to a wind-vane which, unlike the Gianoli system, did not provide sufficient power to correct the course but merely recorded the deviations and transmitted them to an electric motor. Power for this came from alternators driven by screws, rotated at the ends of their shafts by the speed of the boat itself through the water. Self-steering gear was an essential piece of equipment for a boat like *Vendredi 13*. It was no longer 1964 when the winner could overcome all opposition even though his self-steering gear had failed — even if Tabarly was to make history repeat itself in 1976. A steering-gear failure on a boat of *Vendredi's* size would lead automatically to retirement and it would not even be certain that she would be able to make a safe harbour. Details like these underline the inordinate technicalities of these modern boats in which a seaman also has to be an accomplished technician since brute force is not enough to handle them if anything should go wrong. This takes the design of the boat very far away indeed from what Hasler had in mind at the time of the first race. Nevertheless *Jester* was there at the start at Plymouth for the fourth time.

Before the race began, it was realised that the giant mono-hull's number one enemy would be none other than the multi-hull which had been forced to retire from the 1968 race for lack of preparation. The rotating masts on *Pen Duick IV* had been replaced by a more conventional rig and the self-steering gear modified, and then Eric Tabarly had set sail from La Trinité for Fort-de-France, Martinique, in the West Indies, with a crew of two — his faithful companion Olivier de Kersauson, who would later skipper *Kriter II* in *The Financial Times* clipper race round the world in 1975–76, and Alain Colas who had won his racing spurs in the crew of *Pen Duick III* on her Australian voyage.

The trimaran behaved superbly in bad weather and was to notch the amazing average speed of 11 knots on the voyage across. Then it was Panama, California and the Los Angeles–Honolulu Race, when *Pen Duick* showed her stern to the finest Class One boats then afloat, beating *Windward Passage* by a good twenty hours. The trimaran was of but not in the race, which was reserved for mono-hulls, but she had definitely demonstrated how fast she could be. Tabarly with plans for a sixth *Pen Duick* in mind, needed money, but no American seemed interested in purchasing the fantastic boat, since her accommodation below was distinctly sketchy by comparison with the fabulous fittings of most American West Coast yachts. When a sale did not materialise, Tabarly set off for Tahiti, but the yacht's metal struts attaching the floats were showing signs of fatigue, so having effected repairs at Papeete he sailed on to New Caledonia and put in at Noumea. Here Tabarly and Colas split up. They were to sail against one another, first in the Transpacific Singlehanded and then with a crew in the Los Angeles–Tahiti Race. Only after this second contest did Colas make up his mind to plunge head over heels into debt by buying *Pen Duick IV* from Tabarly. Colas set sail for Hobart and then returned to Tahiti before taking this extraordinary aluminium trimaran home to France for the Transatlantic Singlehanded Race. Colas has always kept his objectives firmly in view and he has the ruthless strength of character to achieve what he sets out to do. He now crossed the Pacific and the Indian Oceans with Teura, the girl who was to share his life, and after landing her at Réunion completed the rest of the voyage singlehanded, a matter of 10,000 miles nonstop. *Pen Duick IV* had sailed round the world, changing owners in the Pacific. When he reached La Trinité in Britanny, Colas wrote:

It was over. Day sixty-six had completed a voyage of nearly 10,000 miles, the record singlehanded passage to date. I weighed a ton and my one thought was sleep, but I held on, my eyes puffy with sleeplessness and now I was at the start of the Transatlantic Singlehanded Race.

He was to call the book he wrote after his feat in the 1972 race *Round the World to Victory.*

After boat and skipper had been subjected to such testing, the Atlantic crossing seemed a mere matter of routine. Alain Colas could tell the Race Committee of the Royal Western Yacht Club that he had completed 10,000 qualifying miles, which was better than Tom Follett and even better than Bruce Dalling's 5000 miles in 1968.

After 10,000 miles on the high seas, the boat needed completely refitting before going to the starting blocks for the final sprint. Alain Colas went to Gay's yard at Dinard to prepare his boat.

Derigging the boat was a family affair. The stakes were too high and I did not wish to leave anything to chance. After four years of intensive sailing every single item needed to be checked. The race had become the mainspring of my existence and through it all my ambitions were channelled. I had sacrificed everything to it and mortgaged my future for it. No task therefore seemed too hard if it improved my chances of winning at Newport.

Against *Vendredi 13* and *Pen Duick IV*, two boats of such different design but of equally daring originality, the British fielded a team of traditionally designed boats, except for *Strongbow,* which was a most interesting experiment.

Obviously the man who aroused the greatest interest was Sir Francis Chichester, who had last entered the Singlehanded Race in 1964. At the age of seventy-one he came to the start in a 57-foot ketch-rigged boat. She had been designed by Robert Clark and her main features were reminiscent of Clark's *British Steel.* Chichester had been unwell for some months before the start and the state of his health had even caused anxiety. For many years he had been suffering from a blood disease which damaged his spinal marrow. Despite this he had decided that he was fit enough to make the crossing, a formality for a seaman of his temper. There has been some suggestion, however, with no proof to back it, that Sir Francis knew what a sick man he was and set sail quite deliberately in order to die at sea. From the nature of the man, that seems unlikely. Colonel Odling-Smee of the Royal Western, a long-term friend of Sir Francis, believes it is far more likely that the old mariner thought he could get to Newport safely, even though he knew he was a dying man and though he knew he could not expect to be among the fastest finishers.

He was no stranger to illness and the threat of death, but in all the previous adventures, when he seemed to be in great peril, something had happened to save the situation and Chichester's own strength and vitality had always improved when he got to sea. He was apt to talk of 'miracles'. Colonel Odling-Smee is certain that in 1972 he still hoped that one more miracle would enable him to fulfill his cherished dream of completing the race to Newport before having to resign himself to the inevitable.

Strongbow, skippered by Martin Minter-Kemp who had completed the 1968 race in a trimaran, measured 65-foot long for a displacement of only 8 tons, an unheard of ratio. Even traditionalists, who were somewhat scornful of multi-hulls and thought that mono-hulls still had a lot to offer, were full of enthusiasm for this ultra-light boat. Theoretically she possessed some exceedingly pleasing characteristics — especially her length for speed and a very light displacement which meant her skipper need set only a small proportion of her sail area. But in the final analysis, the boat borrowed elements from both the mono- and the multi-hull and fell badly between them. Her light displacement was to make her puny in heavy seas, and being a mono-hull, her keel slowed her speed and by its weight forced her to carry more sail than a multi-hull. Last but not least, *Strongbow* was to wear her skipper's nerves to shreds since her sails required constant adjustment to the varying strength of the wind. Her light displacement was particularly sensitive to alterations in weather conditions. Despite all this, she was to come in seventh out of the forty boats placed, but there are plenty of experts who thought she could have finished even higher among the leaders. Nevertheless, the design thinking behind *Strongbow* was very similar to Carter's reasoning for the shape of *Vendredi 13* — a long slim hull with plenty of sail power should go very quickly as well as pointing well to windward. It was to inspire other long and narrow hulls in 1976 — *Club Méditerranée* to some extent; Gerard Dijkstra's *Bestevaer,* and Pierre Fehlmann's *Gauloises*. They all had outstanding promise of speed. Sadly, they all fell short of their objectives.

In the British camp there could be no doubt at all about the capability of *British Steel* the 59-foot boat which had sailed 'the wrong way' round the world. Built like a strong-box, of steel, of course, she sailed superbly against the wind as her earlier voyages had proved. Her respectable length meant that she should make a very good time and skipper Brian Cooke could be counted upon to drive her close to her maximum, as he had done with *Opus* in the 1968 race.

Going back to the multi-hulls the French had a second trimaran, *Cap 33*, which was potentially very fast, in which the Brasseries de l'Indochine had sponsored Jean-Marie Vidal, who had previously distinguished himself in the annual singlehanded races organised by the French newspaper *l'Aurore*. In 1968, while still in the New Hebrides where he worked as a chemist, he had made up his mind to enter the 1972 Singlehanded Race. Vidal then made his preparations for the race modestly, but with utter efficiency. Having served in the French forces as pilot, parachutist and frogman, he was undismayed by the thought of battling with the elements in the North Atlantic. He looked a winner without having attracted very much attention from the experts. Since the loss of Joan de Kat's trimaran, newcomers to singlehanded sailing were looked on with some suspicion and despite all his qualities, Jean-Marie Vidal had some difficulty in making his presence felt. I might perhaps mention that his modesty was in striking contrast to the egocentric behaviour of some better-known singlehanders. The person who was to enable him to make his dreams come true was André Allègre, who was to design and build *Cap 33*. He had had a hand in designing *Pen Duick IV* and his ideas on the subject of trimarans were revolutionary. Vidal rightly considered that a big trimaran could travel faster than a monstrous mono-hull like *Vendredi 13*.

Early in 1972 the Race Committee decided to take a firmer line on sponsorship and to alter the current rules accordingly. Vidal was within an ace of having to start again from scratch. *Cap 33 Export* had to be changed to *Cap 33*, while Anne Michaïloff, one of three women to enter, sponsored by the cigarette manufacturers Peter Stuyvesant, had to change the name of her boat *PS*! Meanwhile *British Steel* kept her name as did *Strongbow*, the brand-name of a well-known cider. The Race Committee's word was law, but the rules seemed to be applied more or less strictly according to which side of the Channel the boat has her home port!

Tom Follett had slightly changed direction. This time he came from the Virgin Islands in a large trimaran christened *Three Cheers* because she was the triple-hulled successor to *Cheers*. The boat had been designed by Dick Newick, with all his usual originality, measured 46 feet in length, was built of moulded wood and was supported financially by the third member of the American team, banker Jim Morris. The struts attaching her floats were completely streamlined so that in theory they offered less resistance and formed a pair of wings which made the boat look like some giant ray. The balance of the boat was such that self-steering gear was theoretically unnecessary, and the sail-plan was designed so that the mizzen would balance the canvas on the mainmast, which carried a mainsail, jib and staysail. The moderately sized floats were inclined from the vertical plane to minimise leeway and to work perfectly when the boat heeled. An extra centreboard was fitted in the bows to assist lateral stability, the main centreboard being set slightly astern of amidships. The low aspect ratio rig demonstrated the greatest simplicity. The experience of a man like Follett and the demonstration he had given to the amazement of all in 1968, aroused considerable speculation about the prospects of a trimaran which was more modern than *Pen Duick IV* and incorporated certain improvements from which it was clear that she belonged to the latest generation of multi-hulls.

Comparison of the favourites to win on elapsed time showed that the battle would be between the mono- and the multi-hulls and that never before had the the latter seemed such dangerous opponents. The question was whether *Vendredi 13* would show herself markedly superior despite the lack of time available to prepare her, when faced by the formidable sailing-powers of *Pen Duick IV* skippered by a man who knew every inch of her from the tip of her floats to the top of her mast.

The other unknown factor was the weather. If the competitors were going to have to encounter several of the gales which had blown up in the middle of the last race, they would be better off sailing sturdy mono-hulls. Both from the safety angle, since there was far less danger, and because big mono-hulls could continue to make headway west, and even if their speed were considerably reduced they would be able to cope far more comfortably than the multi-hulls with waves 25 or 30 feet high. Cyclone Brenda, which had sprung up in the Gulf of Mexico during the 1968 race, had made her presence felt with that part of the fleet taking the Azores route, even if she had not endangered it. She had died out in the competitors' path. Nonetheless it is quite easy to imagine that she could have moved further north and caught most of the boats involved. Before August, severe storms are unlikely to affect the routes of the race, even the southerly one, except as freaks. All the same 1968 had shown that, although it had never occurred before, it could sometimes happen that cyclones could move far enough north to constitute a definite danger. Generally they occurred below the fortieth parallel. For all that, Force 9 winds are not really all that exceptional — they often occur close to the Great Circle route (between 10° and 45° west) and off Cape Hatteras.

Taking into account all the unknown factors which are natural con-comittants of the weather conditions, the Singlehanded Race is not won until you reach Newport. Forgetting cyclones for the moment, multi-hulls are bound to put up better performances in moderate and good weather conditions. Furthermore if light winds are unlikely to upset them much, an under-canvassed boat like *Vendredi 13* will be most un-comfortable in light and changeable winds. This is the paradox of this race and what makes it quite unlike any other. The advantages in the route chosen by each competitor will only work in his favour if the weather conditions during the race are right. They can help the odds-on favourite to win or stop her dead in her tracks.

In the small-boat class, Alain Gliksman's *Toucan* seemed extraor-dinarily well suited to win her class. Fortified by his experience of bat-tling on in the 1968 race in a very large ketch, Gliksman had chosen to enter a slim, ultra-light mono-hull, which he could drive virtually to her limits during practically the entire race. She was a converted day sailer designed for lake racing and her three-quarter rig considerably reduced the sail area forward; her headsails were easy to handle and could be changed whenever necessary, while her spinnakers were of a manageable scale. Nevertheless the boat was still very long for her dis-placement and the ratio of sail area was considerable. The major disad-vantage was her very low freeboard which turned *Toucan* into a sub-marine when the waves rose above a certain height. Gliksman, perfectly well aware of the problem, had provided himself with a wet-suit and motor-cyclist's helmet to meet it, settling for the spray rather than for a night and day struggle with great masses of canvas. It needed daring to set sail on so small a craft: the outcome of the race was to prove how right he had been to do so.

Edith Baumann's unfortunate experience in 1968 had not discouraged women from competing and three entered in 1972. On board an Aloa production boat was Marie-Claude Fauroux, a leading dinghy racer who was easily able to translate her experience on small boats into the language of ocean racing. Self-confident and well able to take care of herself, she had what few women have — the steely outlook of the singlehander. The other Frenchwoman, Anne Michaïlof, an experienced ocean cruiser, was on board an aluminium yacht of the Brise-en-Mer type. She reached Newport just in time to be placed. The third woman to enter was a Pole, Teresa Remiszewska, and she chose a 42-foot yawl of traditional design called *Komodor*.

Marc Linski had entered again, in an aluminium boat designed by Dominique Presles, the 48-foot *Isles du Frioul*. This year he had had watertight compartments fitted, 'just in case', and could steer from below decks thanks to the enclosed cockpit and perspex dome on the *Pen Duick II* pattern which allowed him to see what was going on outside while he remained snug and warm. This was a crafty 'extra' which would be much appreciated in the Labrador current where the temperature can drop below zero, and in mid-Atlantic where the helmsman can be soaked by the big rollers.

Guy Piazzini, another of the unlucky ones in 1968, was also at Plymouth in a new boat, a 45-foot Rorqual christened *Cambronne*. Although the boat was fully prepared and superbly equipped, she could not worry the craft specially built for the race. Piazzini was one of that band of competitors, and there are plenty of them, who join the Singlehanded Race to match their boats against the world's best while knowing they have very little chance of winning. The race still produces men who simply want to sail a notable race as well as their physical strength and financial resources permit. Despite the super-monsters lined up at the start, the bulk of the fleet always consists of competitors of this sort ready to sail 'their' race among themselves. That is why so many boats without the slightest chance of winning cross the Atlantic and then make the leisurely cruise home via the Azores. Their skippers do not come home winners, but profoundly changed by the enthralling experience which they have undergone, for which there is no substitute.

Saturday 17 June 1972, and the spectators were massed thickly round Plymouth Sound, its waters cut by the wakes of escorting craft. In the midst of all this coming and going, *Vendredi 13* sailed majestically under her three boomed jibs, apparently handled without difficulty despite her 128-foot length. Wearing a silvery racing driver's helmet, Terlain, a mere pin-head on the gigantic deck, calmly put the helm over

Yves Terlain and his *Vendredi 13* (2). An elegant sail-plan set on three masts so as to provide easy handling for the singlehanded sailor. Designed with great originality to take advantage of water-line length, a major factor in speed under sail. Victory hung on a halyard!

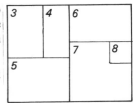

Strongbow, one of the favourites. An interesting attempt to combine an ultra-light displacement with considerable water-line length. If the experiment was admittedly a failure, it was fun finding out!

Marie-Claude Fauroux aboard her *Aloa VII*. She was the first woman past the finishing line at Newport.

Tom Follett's *Three Cheers*. The light winds encountered produced an unusually poor performance. Despite being potentially far faster than *Cheers* in 1968, her time was nearly eleven hours slower.

The ever-faithful *Jester* was sure to be there. Her skipper this year was Michael Richey who steered a course far to the south and took 58 days to finish.

British Steel, the boat which sailed 'the wrong way' round the world. Coming in fourth at Newport, the second mono-hull behind *Vendredi 13*, she was the first British boat home. A fine race and the last one for Brian Cooke (8) who was later lost off the Canaries from the trimaran *Triple Arrow*, a planned entrant for 1976.

An historic moment. On the tenth day of the race, Alain Colas manages to photograph *Vendredi 13* in mid-Atlantic.

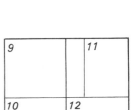

The risk of encountering icebergs is one of the major hazards of the Great Circle route when near Newfoundland.

Cap 33, the trimaran which was to come in third. Her skipper, Jean-Marie Vidal (12) took the southern route.

13. *Gipsy Moth V,* Sir Francis Chichester's last boat. Her skipper proved to be too sick a man to reach America, and was forced to turn back, his son Giles coming aboard to help him.

14. Sir Francis with his wife Sheila. She played a vital role in the life of one of the greatest British seamen of the 20th century.

15. *Toucan,* which Alain Gliksman (16) raced brilliantly into eighth place on elapsed time and confirmed as the fastest 35-footer in the whole race.

17 and 18. *Pen Duick IV*: like a gigantic cobweb hanging in the air this 'floating tennis-court' is still an amazing sight.

19. Alan Colas knocked five days off the record, when, for the first time in the history of the race, a multi-hull was outright victor. This was where *Pen Duick IV* (20) won her spurs and she is still one of the fastest yachts in the world.

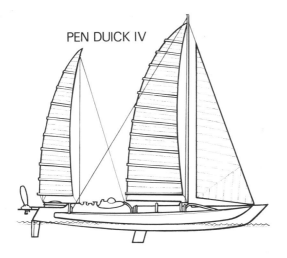

PEN DUICK IV

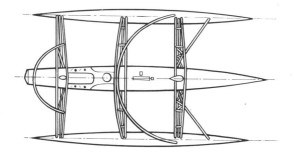

1972—Alain Colas—*Pen Duick IV*—20 days 13 hrs 15 mins

    Length: 67 feet (multi-hull: trimaran)
    Aluminium alloy hull
    Ketch-rigged
    Architect: André Allègre
    Builder: Chantier de La Perrière (France)

and tacked. The bow swung through the eye of the wind without a second's hesitation, the boomed sails swung over to the other tack and the skipper had nothing to do but make sure all was clear ahead. It was a marvellous demonstration and left the spectators awe-struck. Colas had preferred to moor towards the middle of the starting line, but well back as his monster was less handy, and he did not want to take any risks. Meanwhile *Pen Duick IV* tugged at her moorings, her sails shivering, ready to surge forward when her skipper gave the word. As noon drew closer, fifty-two boats were circling waiting for the starting-gun which would signal them to leave the shelter of the Sound and face the rigours of the Atlantic, the moment some of the competitors had been dreaming about for years. It would be the end of the first act, the ending of what had been for all an agonising period of cares, doubts, advice, resolutions, and sometimes of torments shared with those who over the months had become their inseparable working companions. As far as the latter were concerned the play was over, it had given them moments they would never forget and they would sail their boat's race safe at home.

For the singlehanders the second act began at noon with the starting gun. No longer could they rely on others, they had to face each and every problem alone, but first each competitor had to cross the starting line, pass through the breakwater, clear the coast, and set sail for America...

Golden Vanity, skippered by Peter Crowther, was a gaff-rigged cutter built in 1908. She had already crossed the Atlantic four times, but that day she seemed to have strayed in from another world, in which there were still gaff-rigs and where topsails and topsail yards still had some justification. She was last away, sturdily setting sail, the skipper's bicycle rather in the way there on deck, but he wanted it for travelling round America which he was to reach over seventy days later.

Dijkstra's heavy 71-foot mono-hull *Second Life*, was sailing level with *Pen Duick IV*, while *Vendredi 13* was soon setting the pace in front. For a short time Terlain sailed tack for tack with Vidal's *Cap 33*, before slowly but surely drawing ahead. Off the Lizard, the leaders were *Vendredi 13, Pen Duick, Three Cheers,* and Joel Charpentier's big schooner, *Wild Rocket,* which took advantage of a fine seaward tack, but was soon forced back to Plymouth, her sails blown out.

The next day the leaders were past the Scillies, the final danger point off the English coast. The wind began to freshen to 30 knots from the west and soon the entire fleet was sailing close-hauled. Having made up his mind to steer the shortest course along the Great Circle route, Colas sailed *Pen Duick* as close to the wind as he could. During trials he had managed to improve the boat's sailing ability against the wind by tightening a forestay and he could improve it still further. To counter-balance this he had added a third backstay and even though this meant a slight reduction in the area of the mainsail, the boat answered better in the wind.

On board, Colas had installed the weather facsimile machine which he was to keep for his subsequent voyage round the world. This instrument enabled him to locate the areas of low and high pressure and gave him valuable information on weather conditions. Thanks to it he was to be able to plot his course from accurate meteorological observations.

Three days after the start a fresh south-westerly blew up to between

40 and 45 knots and *Pen Duick* was beating close-hauled through walls of water. At about six o'clock in the evening Colas went on deck to take in a reef. While he was working at the foot of the mast, the boat was headed and suddenly recoiled as a wave hit her. The rudder was forced right over and one of the drive shafts from the self-steering gear to the rudder-tab snapped clean through. Colas rushed to the stern knowing that the race was over unless he could mend it. The fact that he knew every inch of his boat was to enable him to save this critical situation. A few minutes later he had taken in all sail and, lashing himself as best he could to the boat, he was up to his neck in water trying to repair the shaft. Luckily he had shipped a few spare parts and two hours later he was under way again under jib and mizzen sails.

> On the evening of 22 June [Colas wrote] the wind dropped, and this must have made Terlain bite his nails . . . This was just what I needed, an alternation of stiff breezes to upset the over-light *Three Cheers*, and light winds in which the giant would remain glued to the water!

On 24 June *Pen Duick*, going hell for leather across the sea, lay to the west of La Rochelle and due north of the Azores.

On 25 June, with the wind gusting to 50 knots, *Pen Duick's* self-steering gear broke down for the second time.

> All the same, I was really rather annoyed when I thought how I had an extra set of everything, sails, halyards, stays, rudder tab, electronic self-steering gear, radio receiver, sextant, steering compass . . . everything had been duplicated except for the vane for the Gianoli self-steering gear, and this had parted in the wind, it had become my too faithful friend over the last four years.

Fortunately the wind moderated and Colas fitted a substitute gear, for although he did not have spare parts for the Gianoli on board, he did have a complete self-steering gear of another make — an Atoms. It was less efficient in strong winds, but worked perfectly in light breezes. Anyway, this gear rescued *Pen Duick* from a very tricky situation.

Here once again was a case of the failure of the self-steering gear on a boat which had just sailed some tens of thousands of miles. Of course the mechanism concerned was extremely sensitive and subject to particularly heavy strain when mounted on a multi-hull. The rapid acceleration of these light craft frequently caused the apparent direction of the wind to change and the force exerted upon the self-steering gear is greater than that exerted upon similar gear mounted on a mono-hull, while the absence of heel exposes them to the full force of the wind. The gear however has to be sufficiently sensitive to operate while the boat is running before the wind, when the speed of the boat often approaches real windspeed and the apparent speed drops almost to zero.

Meanwhile a little further to the south an historic scene was being played out. Everybody who had watched the start at Plymouth had noticed how Sir Francis Chichester had aged. A loose sheet forward had left him momentarily unable to make up his mind what to do. A loose jib was wrapped around the forestay and he had had to rest in the cockpit, suddenly exhausted. It must be admitted that this was a clumsy way to work a boat for a man as accomplished as Sir Francis and the newspapers had seized upon the incident to prophesy the worst. Eleven days after the start a merchant-ship sighted *Gipsy Moth V* under reduced sail and apparently heading back for England. She was then lying about 300 miles west of La Coruña. The next day Chichester made hand signals to an RAF aircraft that he had been taken ill, was proceeding back to England and that all was well on board. On 29 June a radio message revealed that he had asked his son to come to Brest to meet him and had ended with the words 'cold and weak'. Now real anxiety was aroused. The old lion seemed seriously ill.

The French weather-ship, *France II*, took Chichester's message to be a distress signal and headed for his estimated position. Chichester was subsequently to state that although he had told the frigate that all was well, she seemed determined to come alongside. So close did she come, in fact, that clumsy handling brought her into collision with the yacht and smashed the mizzen-mast. A French seaman put the other side of the story when he stated that he was looking down on a listless and exhausted figure sitting in the cockpit and apparently simply wanting to sit there. The swell then smashed the English sailor's yacht against the side of the French weather-ship. Only after this did *France II* launch a boat with an offer of medical assistance. Chichester refused and pointing to his damaged rigging asked them to sheer off. It is hard to establish exactly what happened. Certainly a wrong move was made, but any amateur yachtsman knows that they should only ask the assistance of a large boat in the most extreme emergency. The rigging of a yacht is exceedingly fragile and, with a swell running, a cargo ship will be hard put to come alongside without damaging it. Even if Chichester needed help, the question arises as to why it took so long for a boat to be launched — and Chichester's state of mind may be imagined when he saw the damage to his rigging.

To pile disaster upon disaster, at about two in the morning of 1 July, *France II* ran down an American yacht on passage from Denmark to Spain, when her skipper heard that Sir Francis was in trouble and was sailing towards *Gypsy Moth* in the hope of being able to help. Four survivors were picked up, but another seven went down with the boat. At dawn on that ill-omened day, the Royal Navy frigate *Salisbury* launched a boat and transferred Giles Chichester and several naval personnel aboard *Gipsy Moth* to repair the rigging. Sir Francis, his son and Lt Commander Peter Martin, an experienced yachtsman, remained on board and returned to Plymouth on 3 July. This was the last voyage of this famous seaman who showed a lifelong devotion to sport and adventure. He was sixty-five when he first rounded Cape Horn singlehanded. He died on 25 August 1972 in the Naval Hospital at Plymouth.

Three Cheers had not chosen so southerly a route as *Cheers* and Tom Follett was worried. The expected following winds had not materialised and her average speed was not of the best, being in fact identical with the 1968 time of *Cheers* on a boat potentially much faster. Follett's whereabouts were unknown, since he had no radio transmitter, but he could be presumed to be lying well up with the leaders on the basis of the distances he had run in the first few days of the race. Both Colas and Terlain believed his track to be more southerly than was actually the case and regarded him as their most dangerous rival.

Jean-Marie Vidal in *Cap 33* had headed far to the south in search of following easterly winds. His daily mileage lengthened steadily towards his goal and he had a pleasant smell of the land when he passed Terceira, sailing through the Azores. That evening he watched a splendid sunset gild the peaks of the mountains, rocky fragments set in the Atlantic like buoys to mark the first section of the race. On board all was well, though a few days before the struts to the floats had shown signs of weakness, but he had succeeded in tightening the bolts and so putting the trouble right. While most of the competitors to the north were pressing into the westerlies which raised solid walls of icy water, he was heading for Newport in the sunshine. His track made a wide swell, its lowest point almost touching 37° North, Plymouth lying on the fifty-first and Newport on the forty-second parallel.

Strongbow's progress along the northern route was considerably retarded by foul weather. Into the bargain, Martin Minter-Kemp had injured his knee, which did not help to keep him cheerful when working his boat. He also lost the wind-vane which was designed to power his electric self-steering gear, so he had to spend long hours steering by hand.

Wild Rocket had lost the hatch of her chain-locker and after putting back to Plymouth for new sails and a replacement hatch, bravely set out for the New World once more.

British Steel relished the foul weather. She sailed steadily on close-hauled through the gales which followed one another on the northern route and was judged to be leading the boats whose positions had been reported. Meanwhile Gerard Pestey's *Architeuthis,* that amazing giant catamaran fitted out below decks more like a ballroom than a racing yacht, was reported as leading the boats which had taken the southern track.

Retirements through various causes followed one another day by day, but nobody was quite sure where the three favourites lay and anxiety was beginning to be felt for *Vendredi 13* of which practically no news had been received since the start.

June 26 was the last day on which regular reports were received from boats on the southern route. The weather-ship *France II,* which relayed their positions, had just reported that she was out of range of signals from the competitors. For news of them, reliance would have to be left to chance sightings. *Cap 33* was then leading the boats lying south of the fortieth parallel.

With no news coming from the boats on the southern route, interest shifted to the north, where the wind had moderated slightly. *Vendredi 13* had still failed to report her position, which was rather unusual since she had arranged to send out regular radio messages, but it was soon to be learned that battery failure had caused her a great deal of trouble.

After ten days at sea, the halfway mark for the fastest boats, an extraordinary incident occurred — *Pen Duick* suddenly sighted *Vendredi 13*. Colas saw her round the side of his genoa as she came up over the horizon out there in mid-ocean.

There was Terlain! Two miles ahead playing Peekaboo behind my jib was *Vendredi 13*! It was something you would never have thought could have happened, a chance in a million. I came over the horizon dead astern of him, after ten days at sea, ten days of sailing close-hauled, exactly on the halfway mark, 1455 miles out from Plymouth on the direct track ... It was 3.40 pm and after we had waved to one another I bore away, and our two boats soon drew apart.

The cards had been shuffled once more and dealt out again, but they both knew who had the better hand. If Terlain had been unable to take a decisive lead over the first half of the race in weather conditions which should have suited his boat, he was going to be hard pushed to do it over the second stage when conditions should favour the trimaran. Colas' spirits soared when he thought how he had managed to keep up with the giant mono-hull when sailing close-hauled in winds often from fresh to strong.

On the other hand, Terlain realised he had not driven his boat as fast as she could go and, having competed before, he suspected that weather conditions ahead would not favour him. He had been handicapped by the sheer size of his monstrous boat, which had really needed far longer to prepare her for the race. On craft of that size the smallest accident soon takes on an importance out of all proportion. He had repaired a failure of the self-steering gear but had been unable to replace a number of defective batteries which had thrown out the boat's entire electrical system, preventing him from using his radio transmitter and weather facsimile machine. Also, and this was far more serious when it came to setting the sails, the defective batteries had put the wind-speed and direction indicator out of action as well. In a conventional yacht, these complicated instruments are all extras as it were, but they are vital to boats as big and as long as *Vendredi 13*. Then, on top of it all, he had trouble with the sheaves of the halyards, which made handling the sails an even more complicated task.

Although his chances of winning were seriously affected, he knew the race was only half-run and the game was far from over.

When they met, the two boats were south of the Great Circle Route. A tack to the south-west had forced them to drop in latitude, but after they had parted once again, they were to head north so as to try to lay a course for the American coast to the north of the Gulf Stream.

On 30 June the French space satellite *Eole* fixed the position of *Pen Duick* as 42° 41′W, 41° 04′N. Because of Colas' contractual obligations this news was kept secret. The French Space Research Station located *Pen Duick* each time its satellite passed over the boat, on which equipment had been fitted to emit a continuous signal. This was picked up by the satellite, transmitted to Bretigny and the Doppler factor applied to produce a fix on a purely experimental basis. However, it is by no means impossible that one day such a system should be generally applied to other boats in other races. In the near future satellites could be sent up, programmed to perform such missions for whoever might request them. Any boat equipped to transmit a continuous signal could indicate her position to the satellite and it can be seen how useful this would be not merely to the Race Committee but to the public at large.

In 1972, far more icebergs than usual had been reported and this explains why most competitors were on a track to the south of the Great Circle. *Second Life,* which seemed to be going very well, was the only boat exactly on the Great Circle route. Even *British Steel* had swung slightly to the south, as had *Strongbow.*

There was still no news of *Vendredi 13*'s position on 30 June, when the French satellite had located *Pen Duick IV* at 42° 41′W 41° 04′N. Meanwhile the race was over for *Second Life*: after encountering winds of close on Force 9 she lost her mast, was forced to send out a distress signal and was towed into Newfoundland. The same day the sloop *Lauric* put back to Plymouth which now made 8 retirements, not counting the boats which had managed to set out again.

On 2 July *Three Cheers* was sighted 41° 22′W 42° 29′N which meant that Follett had taken a fairly northerly route and was behind Colas on his westings but ahead of him on his northings. *Pen Duick's* lead became apparent, but *Vendredi 13* still had not reported her position.

Alain Gliksman's *Toucan* had sailed a splendid race, remembering her size, as she now lay 36° 15′W on the southerly route.

In early July Jean-Marie Vidal ran into a bad spell. Having averaged a regular 200 miles a day for several days, he now got stuck in calms which reduced his daily run to between 60 and 80 miles. This forced him north in search of more favourable winds, where he unfortunately encountered the Gulf Stream which perceptibly slowed his rate of progress. Furthermore, the wretched current brought clouds and winds of 35 to 40 knots in place of the calms, thus forcing *Cap 33's* skipper constantly to adjust his sails. The leading boats were now getting close to the American mainland and had to be far more careful in their watchkeeping, the sea-lanes were busier, and there were plenty of fishing fleets about. Nor were they far from those notorious dangers of Nantucket, the shoals and the fogs.

Colas was running before the wind in overcast conditions which had prevented him taking fixes with his sextant. As he neared the Nantucket Light Vessel he decided to round it on dead reckoning and to make his course a little more to the south. Thanks to a brief clearance in the weather he was able to take a fix which showed that he had cleared the Light Vessel by about 30 miles. At this rate he would be into Newport by night, but at about eight on that evening of 6 July the wind dropped and stopped his amazing run, 60 miles or so from the finish.

On 3 July *Vendredi 13* had at last reported her position — 54°W, 43° 30′N. There was no means of knowing if she was ahead of the trimaran, but everything indicated that these two boats were in the lead.

On 6 July, while *Pen Duick* was caught in a flat calm, *Vendredi 13* had the advantage of a favourable tide to take her towards her goal. At 7 pm the Nantucket Light Vessel reported sighting the giant mono-hull, while the trimaran had not yet been seen. It seemed as though Terlain was going to win. If the wind held, he would reach Newport between 8 and 9 pm the next morning. There were only 80 miles between the Light Vessel and the finishing line.

Then came dramatic news — an aircraft had spotted *Pen Duick IV* two hours away from the finishing line. Having rounded Nantucket well to the south, Colas had not been observed: for the last twenty days nobody had picked up his radio signals, and Terlain was the only man to have seen him on the tenth day of the race. At 4.45 pm Colas sighted land. It was Block Island.

'With my big jib set, I was sailing into the setting sun against which the Brenton Tower was silhouetted. The line, I was going to cross the finishing line! There I was all by myself, my chest ready to explode with the tremendous joy which filled it, all by myself as the land gently sucked down the crimson disc of the sun.'

Alain Colas had conquered the Atlantic in twenty days, thirteen hours, knocking five days, seven hours off Geoffrey Williams' record time. It really was a very great achievement which crowned a considerable accumulation of effort and sacrifice. After the tens of thousands of miles she had sailed across the oceans of the world, *Pen Duick* had carried Alain Colas across the Atlantic to well-deserved victory.

The wind let Terlain down, but it sprang up again on the morning of 8 July and *Vendredi 13* crossed the finishing line in second place in a time of twenty-one days, five hours. It is easy to imagine how disappointed Jean-Yves Terlain was, but all the same he had sailed a remarkable race and achieved what had seemed impossible a few months earlier — to steer across the ocean a sailing boat of twice the length and three times the displacement of the previous winners of the race. And the giant craft's original basic plan was to inspire the very man who had just beaten her by sixteen hours!

Third place was very much in the balance. *British Steel* was expected to take it, but it was another French boat, *Cap 33,* which came into Newport next, much to everybody's surprise. Right up to the moment that Vidal took the tow rope cast to him, he believed that he had come in fourth. He was overjoyed to find he was third. It was a great victory for the French, and a slap in the face for the traditional mono-hull! For the first time the multi-hulls, and specifically the two trimarans designed and built in France, had sealed their uncontested mastery of the North Atlantic. Colas and Vidal, and in fairness Tabarly and Allègre as well, could be justly proud of the French effort.

The fourth boat to beat *Sir Thomas Lipton's* record was Brian Cooke's strong-box, *British Steel,* which took the honours of fourth place and was the first British boat home to Newport. Despite the solid build of *British Steel,* Cooke's passage had not been entirely untroubled. A metal tang broke on his mainmast and the outer shrouds collapsed. The skipper was forced to climb the mast in the oily swell that follows a gale and effect jury repairs while the boat swung widely from side to side. He would almost certainly have beaten Vidal home but for that accident.

For the next thirty-five days, boat after boat was to come in, and the last yacht to be placed was Anne Michaïlof's *PS*, taking fortieth place in a time of fifty-nine days, six hours. The American, Tom Follett, was very disappointed, having been so frequently becalmed over the last quarter of the race and having failed to maintain the speed of his 1968 crossing by some eleven hours. Nonetheless he came in fifth.

Bill Howell, skippering *Tahiti Bill* (ex-*Golden Cockerel*), had really bad luck, for just when he was about to finish several hours ahead of Follett, he collided with a Russian trawler and retired when he had to be towed into harbour. He would have been fifth overall and would have beaten Colas for the top place in the multi-hull handicap ratings. It is worth noting here, in view of what has been written earlier about the capsizing of *Great Britain III*, that *Tahiti Bill* survived a bad collision because the damaged port hull of the catamaran was fitted with water-tight compartments, so the sea could only get into one section of one float of the craft. Indeed, Howell was almost able to continue sailing to the finish. A similar collision would almost certainly have sent a mono-hull yacht to the bottom in seconds.

Another surprise was the Frenchman, Gérard Pesty's sixth place in *Architeuthis*, another multi-hull which nobody had expected in so soon. This comfortable craft had really never been designed for a race of this kind and her excellent time of twenty-eight days, twelve hours bewildered a number of the experts. She was an hour ahead of *Strongbow*, whose revolutionary design had led most people to expect better of her.

By his eighth place Alain Gliksman had achieved quite a feat of its kind. His boat, *Toucan*, less than 35 feet in length, had put up the sur-prising time of twenty-eight days, twelve hours, only eight minutes behind *Strongbow*. His success demonstrated how sound his judgement had been in selecting a slim fast boat which could be handled easily. She had shown a clean pair of heels to plenty of other boats which had cost a fortune to build and had needed superhuman efforts to handle!

The first woman home to Newport was Marie-Claude Fauroux of France. Her successful crossing was made in the remarkable time of thirty-two days, twenty-three hours. She proved to her own satisfaction that she could sail the Atlantic singlehanded. Her preparations had been so sound and her equipment brought to such a high working pitch that her boat did not suffer a single failure. She was two days ahead of Yves Oliveaux in an identical boat, although it should be said that he had been handicapped by an injured arm. Of the first seven vessels home, five were multi-hulls, if *Tahiti Bill* is included in their number. Of the two mono-hulls, *Vendredi 13* was in a class of her own and only *British Steel* represented traditional thinking. Thus 1972 was the year of the multi-hulls and specifically of the trimarans — *Pen Duick, Cap 33* and *Three Cheers* being magnificent race-winning machines.

'If I think back to my best run of 3000 miles (Alain Colas had said before the race) I find it was made in twelve and a half days, and if I take my worst, I find it was made in twenty-one or twenty-two days during my voyage round the world. If I take longer, I shall feel disappointed.' This was to show remarkable knowledge of the capability of his boat as well as of his own physique. His performance represents a daily average of 150 miles to achieve this feat, which is no small one when you take into account the weather conditions in the North Atlantic in June. It is hard to think of knocking over five days off a record, and yet this is what *Pen Duick* did — and her design was over four years old. Eric Tabarly was at least proved a prophet in the design of the kind of boat which could win the race, and in bringing so formidable a craft up to her peak of racing efficiency Alain Colas showed enormous reserves of perseverance and courage. To beat such a performance as his, very extraordinary efforts will have to be made, and a great deal of money and hard work will have to go into knocking a few hours off his time, if indeed they can be knocked off. The 1976 race was considerably slower. A giant step forward in yacht design had been made. In the races to follow, no doubt a few hours can be gained by boats designed on the same principles as these big trimarans and gigantic mono-hulls. The weather conditions prevailing when the races are sailed will also have their influence. However, to better the time by a spectacular margin, must surely entail the design of yachts based on different principles and belonging to a new generation of sailing craft still little understood today. As I shall show, Eric Tabarly has tried to solve the problem.

Perhaps the most important lesson to be learned from the 1972 race was that a well-prepared boat is more likely to beat a potentially faster craft which has not had time to work up properly. It was so in 1968 when *Pen Duick IV* was not ready to face the Atlantic. It was so, too, in 1972 when potential greyhounds like *Vendredi 13* and *Strongbow* were eclipsed by proven craft like *Pen Duick IV* and *Architeuthis*.

And it was to prove so once again in 1976, when the monstrous *Club Méditerranée,* with so much potential but not enough sailing time behind her, was beaten home by a yacht one third her size which had been tempered by thousands of miles of ocean racing. One of the committee's new rules for the 1980 race says that not only must boat and skipper have completed a 500 miles qualifying cruise but the boat must also have sailed an additional 1000 miles in open water, fully crewed if necessary. This must help to eliminate the depressing failures by boats which are not really race fit by the time the start gun sounds.

Some may say that the 1972 race was simply a matter of money. They are not entirely right. To win an athletics event, you obviously do not need much financial outlay although you require a great deal of time in training. Obviously, if you are going to race across the Atlantic you will need a boat, and boats, as everybody knows cost money. If the amount needed has risen considerably by comparison with the costs of building the boats for the 1960 and 1964 races, the men who sail them have hardly changed at all. Each of the four winners had a sharply individual character, but it is legitimate to think that their courage and intelligence were points in common. Large-scale sponsorship does not help you to win, it is simply harder to come by, but that does not take anything from the winner's achievement. The winner of the Singlehanded Race will always remain the most cunning, the bravest and the best seaman.

RESULT OF THE 1972 SINGLEHANDED RACE

START: 17 JUNE

		Elapsed Time
1	*Pen Duick IV* ALAIN COLAS (F)	20 days 13 hrs 15 mins
2	*Vendredi 13* JEAN-YVES TERLAIN (F)	21 days 05 hrs 14 mins
3	*Cap 33* JEAN-MARIE VIDAL (F)	24 days 05 hrs 40 mins
4	*British Steel* BRIAN COOKE (GB)	24 days 19 hrs 28 mins
5	*Three Cheers* TOM FOLLETT (USA)	27 days 11 hrs 04 mins
6	*Architeuthis* GÉRARD PESTEY (F)	28 days 11 hrs 55 mins
7	*Strongbow* MARTIN MINTER-KEMP (GB)	28 days 12 hrs 46 mins
8	*Toucan* ALAIN GLIKSMAN (F)	28 days 12 hrs 54 mins
9	*Sagittario* FRANCO FAGGIONE (Italy)	28 days 23 hrs 05 mins
10	*Whisper* JIM FERRIS (USA)	29 days 11 hrs 15 mins
11	*Isles du Frioul* MARC LINSKI (F)	30 days 02 hrs 45 mins
12	*Polonez* CHRIS BARANOWSKI (Poland)	30 days 16 hrs 55 mins
13	*Binkie II* MIKE McMULLEN (GB)	31 days 18 hrs 10 mins
14	*Aloa VII* MARIE-CLAUDE FAUROUX (F)	32 days 22 hrs 51 mins
15	*Flying Angel* JOCK BRAZIER (GB)	33 days 09 hrs 21 mins
16	*Wild Rocket* JOEL CHARPENTIER (F)	34 days 13 hrs 38 mins

17	*Aloa I*	
	YVES OLIVAUX (F)	34 days 17 hrs 30 mins
18	*Cambronne*	
	GUY PIAZZINI (Switzerland)	35 days 10 hrs 24 mins
19	*Concorde*	
	PIERRE CHASSIN (F)	36 days 01 hrs 19 mins
20	*Gazelle*	
	BRUCE WEBB (GB)	36 days 02 hrs 07 mins
21	*La Bamba of Mersea*	
	JOHN HOLTOM (GB)	36 days 04 hrs 30 mins
22	*Blue Smoke*	
	GUY HORNETT (GB)	36 days 21 hrs 26 mins
23	*White Dolphin*	
	WOLF KIRCHNER (W. G)	38 days 07 hrs 17 mins
24	*Ron Glas*	
	JOCK McLEOD (GB)	38 days 09 hrs 50 mins
25	*Shamaal*	
	RICHARD CLIFFORD (GB)	38 days 10 hrs 30 mins
26	*Blue Gipsy*	
	BOB LANCY BURN (USA)	39 days 08 hrs 30 mins
27	*Trumpeter*	
	PHIL WELD (USA)	39 days 13 hrs 25 mins
28	*Mex*	
	CLAUS HEHNER (W. G)	40 days 08 hrs 23 mins
29	*Surprise*	
	AMBROGIO FOGAR (Italy)	41 days 04 hrs 45 mins
30	*Mary Kate of Arun*	
	PAT CHILTON (GB)	41 days 17 hrs 17 mins
31	*Francette*	
	ERIC SUMNER (GB)	43 days 09 hrs 38 mins
32	*Miranda*	
	ZBIGNIEW PUCHALSKI (Poland)	45 days 10 hrs 05 mins
33	*Tinie*	
	HEIKO KRIEGER (W. G)	46 days 15 hrs 30 mins
34	*Scuffler III*	
	JERRY CARTWRIGHT (USA)	49 days 02 hrs 00 mins
35	*Lauric*	
	CHRISTOPHER ELLIOT (GB)	51 days 14 hrs 33 mins
36	*Summersong*	
	ANDREW SPEDDING (GB)	51 days 23 hrs 05 mins
37	*Willing Griffin*	
	DAVID BLAGDEN (GB)	52 days 11 hrs 06 mins
38	*Komodor*	
	TERESA REMISZEWSKA (Poland)	57 days 03 hrs 18 mins

39 *Jester*
MICHAEL RICHEY (GB)   58 days 08 hrs 18 mins
40 *P S*
ANNE MICHAÏLOF (F)   59 days 06 hrs 12 mins

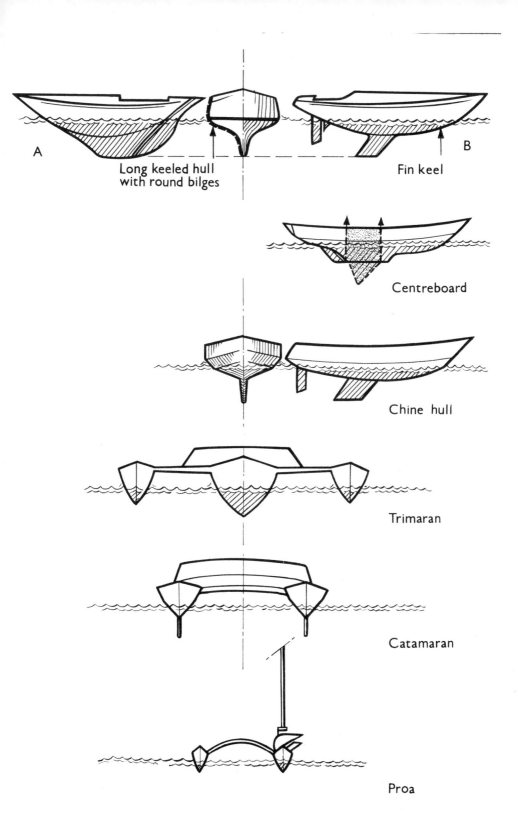

A

Long keeled hull
with round bilges

B

Fin keel

Centreboard

Chine hull

Trimaran

Catamaran

Proa

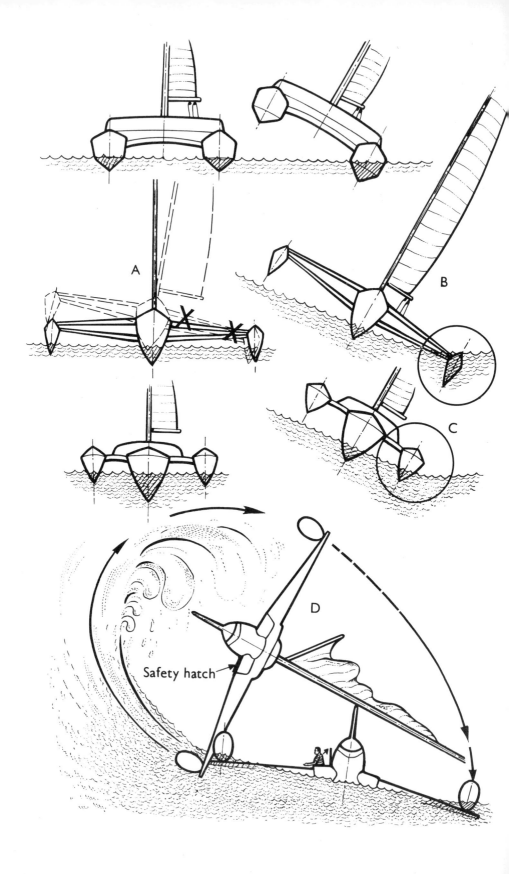

Safety hatch

HANDICAP RESULTS — MONO-HULLS

		Corrected Time		
1	*Blue Smoke*	7days07hrs	06mins	
2	*Blue Gipsy*	9	08	30
3	*Binkie II*	10	13	30
4	*La Bamba of Mersea*	12	09	10
5	*Shamaal*	13	03	10
6	*Flying Angel*	14	07	01
7	*Aloa VII*	14	18	11
8	*Francette*	15	02	18
9	*Whisper*	15	06	35
10	*Willing Griffin*	15	15	46
11	*Ron Glas*	15	19	30
12	*Toucan*	15	22	34
13	*Aloa I*	16	12	15
14	*White Dolphin*	16	14	37
15	*British Steel*	16	18	08
16	*Tinie*	17	01	10
17	*Polonez*	17	09	35
18	*Gazelle*	18	14	07
19	*Mary Kate of Arun*	18	17	17
20	*Sagittario*	19	08	25
21	*Isles du Frioul*	19	16	05
22	*Cambronne*	20	15	04
23	*Mex*	21	01	03
24	*Vendredi 13*	21	05	14
25	*Scuffler III*	21	21	20
26	*Surprise*	22	12	05
27	*Concorde*	22	17	59
28	*Strongbow*	22	21	04
29	*Miranda*	26	10	05
30	*Wild Rocket*	27	06	18
31	*Jester*	27	06	58
32	*Summersong*	28	11	05
33	*P S*	35	10	52
34	*Komodor*	39	01	58

HANDICAP RESULTS — MULTI-HULLS

		Corrected Time		
1	*Pen Duick IV*	16days	19hrs	15mins
2	*Cap 33*	17	10	20
3	*Three Cheers*	19	17	04
4	*Architeuthis*	19	21	35
5	*Trumpeter*	31	15	45

150

CHAPTER SEVEN

~~~~~~

1976–Tabarly Again

Four years had passed since a victorious Alain Colas had crossed the finishing line at the Brenton Tower off Newport in *Pen Duick IV*, the fastest trimaran in the world. In that time ocean racing had taken a tremendous step forward. Yachts had sailed the world's oceans with their crews bent upon breaking established speed records, and singlehanders had set off for fresh seas to sail. Men naturally seek to press beyond the limits of their endurance, going ever farther, ever higher, and accepting ever harder challenges.

In 1973 the first Whitbread Round-the-World Race for fully crewed yachts took place in four stages. The fifteen competitors were away for six months and came home with a rich store of experience. For the first time large racing yachts had faced the stiff west winds of the Indian and Pacific Oceans below the Fortieth Parallel. For the first time since the disappearance of the windjammers a new Cape Horn breed came back to Europe. Hitherto, the only experience of these seas in modern boats had been gained by singlehanders like Chichester and Blyth or by men enthralled by lone cruising like Moitessier in his *Joshua* or Poncet and Janichon in *Damien*, but no real race for crewed boats had been sailed on such a track below the three great southern capes. It was a revelation and the boats stood up to conditions far better than anyone had imagined at the start. Of course several were dismasted, others suffered rudder damage and there was the tragic loss of three lives. Sad as this may be, one has to remember that such accidents were part of the daily round in the old days of the windjammers. Eight men, after all, were washed overboard from *Fleetwing* in the 1866 Transatlantic Race. The material side of the balance sheet remained in credit, since all the yachts which started the Whitbread, finished the race, which close examination of the design of one or two of them would not have led one to presume. They showed amazing potential under sail, by comparison with the windjammers, despite the violence of the elements.

The winner of the race, *Sayula II,* was a stock Swan 65 ketch, which shows that production boats from the best yards are built to very

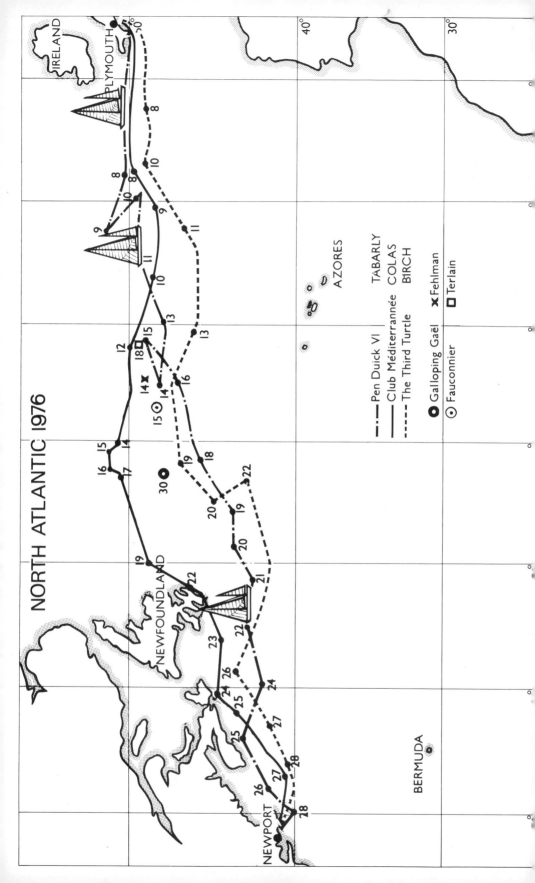

exacting standards these days. She had some minor problems, of course, but she kept going safely and quickly in the most notoriously stormy oceans of the world — though most of her crew would not want to experience again the one serious knock-down she suffered in the roaring forties.

The British Navy's entry *Adventure* was also a stock boat — a Nicholson 55 — and she performed extremely well in the handicap ratings, too. Fastest around the world was the one-off big ketch *Great Britain II,* skippered by Chay Blyth and crewed by British paratroopers. Her expected battle with the big French entry did not materialise because Tabarly's 73-footer *Pen Duick VI* lost her mainmast twice before she eventually completed the circuit. Throughout her entire voyage round the world, *Pen Duick VI*, for instance, was only forced to heave to once, off New Zealand. The competitors continued to make way even in the very strong westerlies of the roaring forties, particularly in the Indian Ocean, where weather conditions were by far the worst of the entire race.

A second round-the-world race started from England in 1975. This was *The Financial Times* Clipper Race — a circumnavigation with only one port of call on the way, and was the occasion on which *Great Britain II* and *Kriter II* beat *Patriarch's* record, which had stood since 1870.

In 1973, Alain Colas had seized the opportunity to complete a singlehanded voyage round the world at the same time as the Whitbread race was run, and to push his trimaran to her very limits. For safety reasons the Committee of the Whitbread Round-the-World Race did not accept multi-hulls as entrants — it was impossible, too, to handicap them with mono-hulls. Colas decided to set sail in his trimaran when the race started and to sail round the world south of the three southern capes. His performance cannot be compared with the mono-hulls which each shipped a crew and which put in at Cape Town, Sydney and Rio de Janiero, while Colas only stopped at Sydney. Nevertheless, his voyage was a real 'first' for a multi-hull. The boat had been modified to stand up to the mountainous seas which she would meet round Cape Horn and in the roaring forties, and although her performance was slightly reduced in consequence, she was a much safer boat. One of the main modifications was that the bows of the central hull and the two floats were enlarged to prevent her burying her nose in a heavy sea. Colas rechristened his ocean-goer *Manuréva*, and although she did not break *Patriarch's* record, a passage round the Horn by a multi-hull was an event which gave the lie to a fair number of over-hasty prognostications and rather upset the ideas of some of the traditionalists of seamanship under sail. One should also remember that the British husband-and-wife team, Colin and Rosie Swale, had already sailed round Cape Horn in their 30-foot cruising catamaran *Anneliese* — an exploit which surprised many of the anti-multi-hull faction.

The only deep motive behind Colas' two-stage round-the-world voyage was the search for sailing performance and the exploit itself. All the same what he did deserves respect because of the sheer scale of the achievement and the fact that it was accomplished by the outright winner of the 1972 Singlehanded Race. This round-the-world voyage also gave Colas the chance to think very hard about the next Singlehanded Race, to get to know his wonderful sailing machine still better and to continue his duel with the elements. The fruits of this thinking were to help him later to choose the boat which he hoped to sail to victory in 1976. The Round-Britain Race for two-men crews, in which he was to compete with his brother, Jean-François, in July 1974, was to crystallise for him the choice of a giant mono-hull.

Having won the 1972 Singlehanded Race, and sailed round the world south of the three southern capes, Alain Colas and his *Manuréva* were to seek a fresh venture. This time it was a race for two-men crews in five stages round the British Isles. For Colas, this meant the chance of measuring the performance of his boat against such massive mono-hulls as Leslie Williams' *Burton Cutter*, or the giant catamaran, *British Oxygen*, raced by Robin Knox Johnston and Gerry Boxall, the power-boat record-holder and racing driver. The multi-hulls were to come out conquerors in this race, *British Oxygen* winning from boats which had already caused a stir in the 1972 Singlehanded Race and which were to come to the start again in 1976. *Three Cheers* was the boat which caused the winner most concern, making up time on the second and fifth legs of the race to come in second. Third was *Gulf Streamer*, another trimaran from the drawing-board of Dick Newick, designer of *Cheers* and *Three Cheers*. Very soon all three multi-hulls were entered at Plymouth for the fifth Singlehanded Race, and undoubtedly at that time they were the three fastest boats in the world. *Manuréva* finished the Round-Britain fourth, without having come to the front in any of the five legs of the race. Since her return from her round-the-world voyage, she had felt the effect of all the extra weight aboard and her sailing performance had undoubtedly been below her capabilities. But Alain Colas came to the conclusion that he had taken the multi-hull about as far as she would go.

When you know you are going to win the Singlehanded Race [Colas was to write] it is like a volcano erupting. It hits you right between the eyes! You know you are going to go in for it again . . . If I was to win in 1976, I knew I could not stand still. *Manuréva* had reached her peak and other multi-hulls had begun to come up and join her, as I saw in the Round-Britain Race. It was obvious that boats like *British*

Oxygen and *Gulf Streamer* were now matching the sailing performance of *Manuréva*, and I was certain that to win the Singlehanded Race, I should have to beat the 1972 record. This called for a passage of eighteen days. Now that all the questions had been answered, there seemed little incentive to build another multi-hull ... I had been fourth in my last race, but even if I had come in third, second or first, it would not have altered my decision.

From that moment Colas made up his mind — to build a giant mono-hull. Her length would be even greater than that of *Vendredi 13*, but her characteristics would be based on the same principle, that of exploiting her water-line length. Colas had been enormously impressed by *Vendredi 13* in the 1972 Singlehanded Race. Had she been fully prepared for the race, she should have beaten *Pen Duick IV*. Furthermore, he felt that *Manuréva* was almost old-fashioned, even by comparison with the multi-hulls which had beaten her in the Round-Britain Race. His thinking was to lead to the design of an enormous four-masted sailing-vessel 236 feet long. The conqueror of the Atlantic intended to use the same sail-plan which he had learned to master, but to multiply it as many times as were needed to propel a mono-hull of such great length. 'Since 2000 square feet was the limit of the sail area which I could handle, I had to divide this area by four, into separate components.'

At the beginning of the planning stage, Colas had thought it would be more advantageous to have only three masts and a shorter water-line length than was decided later.

When we studied the problem in greater depth [Colas explained] we soon saw that she would be carrying too little canvas. We should then have had to increase it and this would have resulted in each of the sail-plans interfering disastrously with the other. The masts would have had to be taller to carry a greater sail area, and this was the last thing I wanted. The rig had to be spaced out and so the length of the boat had to be increased. The naval architect in charge of the project was Michel Bigoin, and he should take the credit for making the breakthrough to 236 feet. From his slide-rule and his calculations, it became apparent that it was much better to have a fourth mast and not to go beyond a certain size of sail and thus to obtain the sail area needed to propel a boat of the optimum water-line length in relation to the propulsive force ... Finally we settled on four sloop-rigged masts set in the most advantageous position.

Alain Colas reached these conclusions in March 1975 in the middle of his do-or-die battle to raise financial backing and while he was working out the hull shape of the giant boat.

Race rules allowed competitors to be sponsored, provided that the boat concerned did not carry the commercial name in a way offensive to good taste. In fact, the sponsored boat could not display any mark or slogan identified with the sponsor except for the boat name, and that name could not in any event be more than twenty letters long. Realising the assistance which commercial sponsorship could lend competitors, the Royal Western Yacht Club allowed such sponsorship without losing sight of the original concept of the race, which was first and foremost a sporting event.

Thanks to this clause, 1976 saw sponsorship breaking out all over. Businessmen had the Atlantic winds in their nostrils, and for some competitors the first race was going to be the race to raise financial backing. Although Colas had been much impressed by Terlain's success with Claude Lelouch, in 1975 he could be proud of having been able to launch his own boat, thanks in large measure to the support of the Club Méditerranée. The press-office which supplied information on the giant's preparation and race performance to the French provincial press, in direct challenge to the national newspapers, was the result of an extraordinary piece of organising on Colas' part. Each newspaper in the commercial group gave Colas advertising space. This he 'sold' to Club Méditerranée to raise the cash needed for the boat. He also fed the group news of the project ahead of the rest of the press. This meant that with provincial newspaper support he was able to ensure that his backers could publicise their part in the operation. Detailed information on the whole project was fed to the eighty provincial newspapers. It is only to be hoped that this exclusive exchange of news and advertising matter would satisfy both parties until the boat came home to Newport. Colas' image and that of the Club went well together. As he said: 'For both the Club and me, travel, the wide open spaces, sport and the sea join in chorusing a hymn of joy in living and physical well-being.'

But in 1976 the sponsors did not confine their bets to the favourites. This was to be the race of the free press mention of names like Club Méditerranée, *Old Moore's Almanack*, Robertson's Jam, Croda, Logo, Kriter, Patriarch, Nova-Pronuptia, Gauloises, ITT Océanic, Kervilor, Petit Breton, Keep Cap d'Agde, Ackel France, Unibrass, Britanny Ferries, *Financial Times*... Apart from ethical considerations, a groundswell of criticism arose in France, accusing the sponsors of diverting to the race funds normally allocated to conventional publicity. For this reason French national radio and television networks decided not to give the names of the boats during the race. It was a matter of trying to make the sponsors become genuine patrons once more!

Although this system of sponsorship may have shocked the

traditionally minded, it must be admitted that it has enhanced the sporting side of the race. Without the advertisers, the Singlehanded Race would not enjoy its present wide popular appeal, but the proviso must be made that the spirit of the race must be preserved.

Meanwhile the runner-up in 1972, Jean-Yves Terlain, was quietly organising his entry. Many people, and particularly the British, were surprised when the official list of entrants announced that he was competing in *Kriter III* (ex-*British Oxygen*). Terlain had gone to the West Indies for the last three years to charter his giant mono-hull, *Vendredi 13*, on charter, and here he was popping up again with a *catamaran,* while Colas had gone quite the other way about things and had changed from trimaran to mono-hull. There was every reason to be surprised. The Atlantic alone would decide the struggle which was now brewing.

Terlain had his eye on what was then the biggest catamaran in the world but the debts which he still had to pay before he became outright owner of *Vendredi 13* forced him to be realistic.

However, the president of Kriter-Patriarch, Monsieur Boiseaux, was to give Michel Etévenon the means to settle the financial problems, having already backed the round-the-world voyages of two earlier *Kriters*. So Terlain was to be in the fifth Singlehanded Race with *Kriter III*.

The two hulls of this mighty craft, each fitted with a keel, measured 70 feet in length and the mast was 90 feet high. The area of the mainsail was 1000 square feet and that of the genoa 1500. Remembering her small displacement, this was an enormous sail area, generating boundless power, so that in ideal conditions the boat could hit twenty-five knots. And this is where the trouble lay. The ratio of sail area to displacement is what makes catamarans capable of such terrific performance: it is also what undermines their stability and makes them such a safety risk, particularly since they only have two hulls. With no ballasted keel to hold them down, catamarans can be capsized by a sudden beam wind. Risks must therefore be taken when skippering such a craft across the Atlantic hell-bent on winning. In 1972 we saw how trimarans dominated the race. The first catamaran would have come in fifth if it had not collided with a trawler. This was Bill Howell's cruising boat. *Kriter III* had little in common with *Tahiti Bill's* spacious accommodation and she was certainly far faster, yet how would she behave in the heavy seas which she was bound to encounter if she chose the Great Circle route? Terlain had twice sailed the race, so he was in a good position to guess how she would perform. Nevertheless, he must have known the risks involved in sailing this type of boat.

Time was undoubtedly Terlain's trump-card. The boat was ready in all respects and had been sailing for the past two years. Her designer, Rod McAlpine-Downie, had called in engineers from the British Aircraft

Corporation to strengthen the spars which carried the enormous pressure exerted by the mast set over the water. Red White, director of Sailcraft, the yard where she was built, and who was to win the Olympic Gold Medal for Britain in the Tornado catamaran class later in 1976, took Terlain in hand to demonstrate the extraordinary boat to him. The latter sailed his qualifying 500 miles from England to La Rochelle and he made this French port his base before the start of the race. Being able to train and having the time free in which to do it instead of being forced to work on the boat right up to the last minute, was no mean advantage, particularly if you mean to win. When people claimed that she had never been built for singlehanded ocean-racing, Terlain would remind them of her astonishing runs in the Round-Britain Race, when weather conditions had not always been particularly kind. Her best run had been 470 miles in forty-three hours and what better could be said than that? However, it should not be forgotten that she would have the other big multi-hulls on her heels, and that if they encountered deep depressions, the trimarans, with their extra hull to give them a considerable extra margin of safety, would be able to drive on harder than *Kriter III*. One could only hope that Terlain would have such confidence in his boat as to be able to push her to the limits and discover just how far he could go with her. Eric Tabarly gave this opinion of the giant catamaran:

> I do not think the boat can sail a faster Atlantic passage than the two trimarans *Great Britain* and *Grand Large*, which Gliksman has thought of having designed for him by Allègre. Of course the boat is capable of high speed in sheltered waters but she is potentially far less comfortable in heavy seas. I am not all that sure either how structurally sound she is, and I should not be happy if I were on board her. I think there is a definite safety hazard in entering the Singlehanded Race in a catamaran.

It is interesting to know the views of a man whose thinking lay behind the design of *Pen Duick IV* and who has such a thorough knowledge of the North Atlantic.

Vendredi 13 was to be at the start once more renamed *ITT Oceanic* — news which pleased quite a lot of people. Of course, she was somewhat outmoded technically for she was four years old, but this time she was to be completely ready for the race. The accommodation fitted below decks had increased her all-up weight, but it could be assumed that her blocks would turn, that her electrical system would work properly and so would her self-steering gear. Her skipper, Yvon Fauconnier could be relied upon, since he had sailed in her for several years and therefore knew her well enough to get the best out of her. Fauconnier had been a notable ocean-cruiser in his time, but he had often shown that he was a highly competitive ocean racer and had skippered an Arpège to class victory in the RORC championship. This was important since racing experience is vital if anyone is to have any chance of winning so hard and ruthless a race.

Among the mono-hulls challenging for victory in the big boat class, *Pen Duick VI* posed as big a threat. While racing in, and winning, the Atlantic Triangle Race in 1975–76, Eric Tabarly had made up his mind to take the sixth of his *Pen Duick's* to Plymouth, although the 73-foot boat had been designed to the IOR rating and for a crew of at least fifteen, but Tabarly had modified the heavy winches on the boat so as to be able to raise the foresails singlehanded. The news electrified the specialist world of ocean racing. They knew the proven qualities of the boat and they knew that her skipper was the only man capable of sailing her successfully. *Pen Duick VI* was a formidable competitor especially when it was remembered that Tabarly had crossed the Atlantic in 1974 to reach the start in Bermuda in a record time of sixteen days. Admittedly then, Tabarly had had a full and fully trained crew, but he had not been racing.

Tabarly completed his qualifying 500 miles for the 1976 Race off Brazil before setting out on the third leg of the Atlantic Triangle. He averaged 170 miles a day without pushing the boat and without self-steering gear. In March 1976, he had remarked:

Since I have no other boat at my disposal, and in the absence of anything better, I intend to race *Pen Duick VI*. She is not the ideal boat for the Singlehanded and she was not built for it. Being a mono-hull she does not have the speed of the multi-hulls, and even when sailing close-hauled there is nothing to show that she will do better than *Great Britain III*. Furthermore she is going to be very hard to handle singlehanded. A boat like her is very sensitive to the set of her sails, and there are therefore bound to be very many adjustments of her headsails. Each one demands the expenditure of so much energy that, when you add the physical effort of tacking on top of it, this Atlantic crossing may well turn into an endurance test. *Great Britain III* will be just as hard to work, but at least she will sail faster. I should certainly prefer to have the trimaran at my disposal.

But if you imagine Tabarly thought he was beaten before he had even started, then you do not know your man at all! If he had made up his mind to challenge a fleet of boats specially constructed for the race, it meant that he thought he had some chance of winning. This was the only explanation for the action of an outstanding seaman who had spent most of his life trying to sail faster and faster, and to beat his own best performance at the same time as he conquered his opponents.

A member of the audience at a lecture he gave a month before the race had asked him what sort of weather conditions he would like during the event. Like a flash he had replied: 'Plenty of head winds and plenty of strong winds.' In extreme conditions he knew that his perfectly tuned boat would have the advantage over prototypes and the super-fast but tender multi-hulls. Finally, Tabarly was a fighter with enormous powers of physical endurance, and foul weather brought out those qualities.

The trimaran *Great Britain III* also seemed formidable. One of the latest designs of the British designer, Derek Kelsall, she had been built for Chay Blyth's sponsor Jack Hayward by Bayside Marine. She was to be skippered by Blyth and, if he had never taken part in the Singlehanded Race before, he had some impressive achievements behind him — he had rowed across the Atlantic, sailed the 'wrong way' round the world singlehanded and had skippered *Great Britain II* to elapsed time honours in the Whitbread Round-The-World in 1973. His physical fitness and seamanship could be relied upon to handle one of the biggest trimarans in the world, measuring 80 feet in length, 40 feet at the beam and displacing eighteen tons. In fact the latest trimarans were proportionately far lighter and, according to her designer, *Great Britain III* had been designed for the proposed multi-hull criss-cross race across the Atlantic, planned for 1973, but it was cancelled for lack of entries.

But an annoying accident occurred at the end of Blyth's 500 qualifying miles, which could have proved tragic and resulted in the death of this famous skipper. *Great Britain III* came into collision with a cargo ship in the Channel and the stem of the port float was shattered. Despite the Force 8 wind the damaged trimaran managed to draw away safely but an hour later she heeled over and capsized. Within forty minutes Blyth had been picked up by a British trawler which managed to tow *Great Britain III* back to Plymouth. Later she was righted and repaired and a new mast was stepped.

However, a second obstacle proved too much for the big trimaran. The accident had given Blyth's insurers second thoughts and her owner, Jack Hayward, had to scratch her. As he explained: 'No insurer will take the risk, except Lloyds, and they will only cover her for half her value.' So one of the favourites was to remain in harbour.

While still on the subject of multi-hulls, *Gulf Streamer*, from the naval architect Dick Newick who designed *Cheers*, capsized in April 1976 on her way to England for the Singlehanded Race in which she was due to start with sail number one. After four and a half days her crew of two was picked up by a container-ship: the skipper Philip Weld, who was to have taken the helm during the race, and the crewman, had had to live as best they could in the waterlogged upturned hull. It seems the accident was caused by a rogue wave of over thirty feet which stood the boat on her beam ends, while a second wave turned her over completely.

160

Following her launch in 1974, *Gulf Streamer* had already crossed the Atlantic twice, notably with a passage of seventeen days when she had come over to take third place in the Round-Britain Race.

Philip Weld had had every expectation of being among the leaders at Newport in 1976. His amazing craft displaced six tons for her length of 60 feet so she was ultra-light. Once again weight is the enemy of multi-hulls, although they must be heavy enough not to take off!

Kelsall and Newick are currently the principal designers responsible in England and America for experimenting in high-performance multi-hulls. Although neither of their large boats was able to start in the 1976 Singlehanded Race, we shall see that their smaller designs performed miracles. In fairness, the Frenchman Allègre should be linked with their names, who helped to design the 1972 winner, *Pen Duick IV,* and who designed and built *Cap 33* and *Grand Large*, both of which were entered for the 1976 race.

However, the number of boats scratching before the start of the race continued to mount. Jean-François Colas, Alain's brother, had entered *Manuréva*, which had won when she had been called *Pen Duick IV*. He successfully completed his 500 qualifying miles, only to be confined to a French harbour by the discovery that metal fatigue had taken its toll and the big trimaran was no longer truly seaworthy.

Grand Large hit the headlines for several months before she, too, was stuck in a French port. She was a most exciting craft, capable of giving *Great Britain III* a very hard race indeed if the latter had managed to start. Launched on 2 April, the boat was immediately rigged for her qualifying 500 miles, which she sailed at an average speed of 11 knots, which makes one wonder what her true sailing potential would have been. Revolutionary methods of construction had managed to give her a displacement of 11 tons and an identical pair of masts carrying a maximum of over 2300 square feet of canvas between them. An average speed of 8 knots between Plymouth and Newport was the record to beat, and it was fair to assume that here was an excellent tool for out-right victory. However, a serious disagreement arose between Pierre English and Alain Gliksman, each claiming the right to skipper her singlehanded, and this eventually immobilised her under a flurry of writs. The climax of the sorry story occurred when she was hoisted out of the water and apparently split, revealing certain distortions due to the hull-construction. Here was the combination of a backer thinking he could conclude a successful advertising campaign, two competent skippers, and a legal tangle which had nothing whatever to do with sport. Whose fault was it?

There remained *Cap 33*, the trimaran which the Frenchman Jean-Marie Vidal had sailed into third place in 1972. In 1976 she was to be skippered by the American, Thomas Grossman, and the experts considered her a potential winner on elapsed time. Finally mention should be made among the boats entered for the Pen Duick Trophy (for the largest boats) of *Spirit of America,* skippered by Michael Kane. She was a 62-foot trimaran, displacing six tons and designed by the Australian, Lock Crowther. She had apparently reached the astounding speed of 25 knots over slightly more than the measured mile.

In 1976 three equal trophies were offered for the first time; thus giving the little boats their chance. The Jester Trophy, named after the boat belonging to the creator of the race and the only yacht to have taken part in all five races from 1960 onwards, was to be awarded to the skipper of the first boat home with an overall length of 38 feet or under and a water-line of 28 feet.

The Gipsy Moth Trophy would be given to the skipper of the first boat home with a water-line length of between 28 and 46 feet, and this was named in memory of *Gipsy Moth*, in which Sir Francis Chichester had won in 1960 and come second in 1964.

Finally the Pen Duick Trophy would be awarded to the skipper of the first boat home with a water-line length of over 46 feet. It commemorated *Pen Duick II* the 1964 winner and *Pen Duick IV*, winner in 1972.

It must, however, be admitted that the battle of the giants was the most interesting and that this was what the public at large followed. Would the record time of twenty days, thirteen hours be beaten? All the same the marked interest in the smaller boats in 1976 was understandable, since they comprised over half the fleet. From start to finish this 'race within a race' was going to be exciting to follow.

Marc Linski was among the favourites for the Jester Trophy. I have described how his boat sank in 1968. Despite this he took part in the 1972 race, and came in eleventh. In 1976 he had entered a boat specially designed for the race by the Marseilles naval architect, André Mauric. Five of these Frioul 38 Class boats were to start, each skippered by an instructor from Linski's sailing school. On their return from Newport they would be used as training ships. Yves Olivaux, Guy Cornou and Bernard Pallard had each chosen the same type of boat, a Melody, in which to compete, while Gilles Vaton, one of Mauric's designers, had himself shared in the development of a boat built specially for the Jester Trophy in moulded wood. From America, Mike Flanagan brought a 38-footer specially designed by Dick Carter, and the English girl sailor Clare Francis had entered an Ohlsen 38, *Robertson's Golly*.

In opposition to this flotilla of mono-hulls, a number of little multi-hulls had been tuned to try to carry off the trophy for their class. At all levels the Singlehanded Race is a battle between mono-hulls and multi-hulls. Among the multi-hulls — all trimarans — the most formidable were the British favourite, the Kelsall-designed *F T, Nova*, skippered by the Frenchman Eugène Riguidel, and the three 31-footers designed by Newick and skippered by two Americans and a Canadian. Any one of a number of unknown singlehanders could reveal their qualities for the first time, and win, for the Singlehanded Race has the magical attraction of setting men of totally different ways of thinking against one another on one of the most difficult oceans of the world.

There were some forty competitors for the Gipsy Moth Trophy and the odds-on favourite was the Briton, Mike McMullen, in *Three Cheers*, the name of a boat which has so constantly recurred, and the logical development of *Cheers*, so brilliantly raced by Tom Follett in 1968. In the 1972 race, McMullen had made a passage of thirty-one days on the 32-foot sloop, *Binkie II*, and this time he had a formidable craft in a trimaran tuned to racing pitch. A self-steering gear powered from solar panels had been fitted and the twin centreboards, judged ineffective, had been replaced by a central plate. This wonderful boat had finished only one hour and eleven minutes behind *British Oxygen* at the end of the gruelling Round-Britain Race, which gave some idea of her potential. Even with her comparatively slight length of 46 feet she could challenge for first place on elapsed time, having averaged 200 miles a day on a voyage from the Hebrides to Cornwall. This would be McMullen's second Singlehanded Race and he had had considerable experience in multi-hulls. His nearest challengers were *Quest*, the 54-foot winner of the 1976 Crystal Trophy, and *Toria*, which had competed in the Round-Britain Races of 1966 (which she won), 1970 and 1974 and, as *Gancia Girl*, had finished seventh in the 1968 Singlehanded Race. In fact, as we shall see, most of the multi-hulls had already competed in the Round-Britain Race and the Crystal Trophy, which are the only major races open to that type of boat in Britain and provide a real testing ground for catamarans and trimarans designed to compete in the Singlehanded Race.

There was no lack of serious contenders for the Gipsy Moth Trophy among the mono-hulls and mention should be made of *Gauloises* nicknamed *Super-Toucan* because she was a logical extension of the boat which Alain Gliksman had used to win the 1972 class for boats of under 35 feet. A slender thoroughbred, lying low in the water, carrying plenty of ballast and plenty of canvas, she was a craft with formidable qualities when sailing into the wind. Her nearest challenger was *Bestevaer,* inspired by *Strongbow*, but aluminium-built at Huisman's yards. Measuring 54 feet, she was designed to sail into the eye of a stiff breeze. Her skipper, Dijkstra, was no novice as he had sailed the huge *Second Life* in 1968. Mention should also be made of two French boats, *Arauna IV* a hard chine wooden boat built by the Costantini Brothers and *Pétrouchka*, ex-*Isles du Friuol*, Linski's boat in 1972.

To oppose this fleet, Alain Colas had entered his gigantic 250-tonner.

From the moment he decided to enter the 1976 race, and despite his serious accident in the port of La Trinité in May 1975, he had never had the slightest doubt of the soundness of the whole vast operation which he had undertaken. He would have received plenty of sympathetic understanding if he had decided to give up the whole thing after the accident, for it was serious enough to deter all but the most singleminded. It happened aboard *Manuréva*. An anchor line caught around Colas' leg and almost severed it. He was in hospital for months and for a long time there was a real fear that the foot could not be saved. However, the limb began to mend and Colas continued undaunted with his ambitious plans from a hospital ward that looked more like a top executive's office. Thanks to the backing of the Club Méditerrannée, which had given its name to his boat, his financial worries were partly resolved. Physically his health was improving daily and there was every expectation that he would get to the start, handicapped it is true, but quite fit enough to handle his boat. He was also able to complete his qualifying distance in the months before the start while his boat was being worked up. A vessel of her size can only be handled by the singlehander with one fundamental proviso — that none of the equipment fails. 'Technology has reached such a pitch,' Colas calmly reported, 'that nowadays nothing is impossible. I am the slave of technology.' It is easy to understand the importance of race preparation for a boat conceived on such a superhuman scale. It is essential that everything should have been thought of — taking in a reef, setting a sail, lowering an anchor, all the constant and traditional activities of a normal boat translated to this monster. To go through a simple 'Check-list' of the gear on board a boat of this size takes some time when one is singlehanded — and that's provided there's no hitch.

The research behind the building of the largest four-masted yacht in the world today is itself an interesting study. Surprisingly enough the hull shape is traditional enough, her deck plan sensible and only her length would categorise her as a monster. She has an elegant counter and her keel is very narrow for a craft of her size. Unlike *Vendredi 13*, her hull has some tumble home and is proportionately broader in the beam. Her designer, Michel Bigoin, thought that her average angle of heeling would be about 12 degrees. Her ballast is slightly less than a third of her displacement and comprises 60 tons of depleted uranium 238. Here is one of the biggest uses of waste matter and its recycling in the world. *Pen Duick VI* was the first yacht to use depleted uranium, with a much higher density than lead, as ballast. It is easy to see the advantages of such technology. In addition to lowering the centre of gravity, the main effect is to produce a slimmer profile and to reduce the area of wetted surface, the two principal factors in slowing a boat through the water. Once the plans had been drafted it remained to see

1. Start of the big boat class in Plymouth Sound. An armada of spectator boats surrounds the giant *Club Méditerranée*. The big ketch on the right is *Pen Duick VI* which has lost no time in tacking on to port to draw ahead of the giant.

2. *Club Méditerranée* creaming along under full sail.

3. On 9 June she was seen by the container ship *Atlantic Cognac*. A broken halyard had dropped one sail into the water and the fourth jib had been carried away by the violence of the wind.

4. Alain Colas examines one of his broken halyards.

5. Clare Francis aboard *Robertson's Golly*.

6. Geoffrey Hales, the British competitor who won the Handicap trophy in *Wild Rival*.

7. In Newfoundland the mainsail of *Manureva* was used to replace the ripped sail of *Club Méditerranée*.

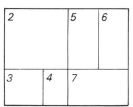

8. Jean-Yves Terlain and Yvon Fauconnier on board the lifeboat which took them to the Russian tug after they had left their boats.

9. *Gauloises*, which Pierre Fehlmann had to abandon before it sank.

10. *Kriter III*, one of the latest designs of ocean-going catamaran, was also destined to sink in the north Atlantic during the race.

11. Jean-Yves Terlain prepares to abandon ship.

12. One of the favourites, *Spirit of America*, turned back to Plymouth on the 11th day after suffering a number of problems.

13. Yvon Fauconnier holds the bent winch handle which injured his arm and leg so badly that he was forced to give up the race. He had to watch impotently as the storms roared over *ITT Oceanic*.

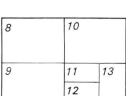

14	17	18
15	16	19	20

14. David Palmer celebrates his arrival in *Financial Times* with his wife and Colonel Odling-Smee of the Royal Western Yacht Club

15. Daniel Parisis was first in the Gipsy Moth Class with *Petrouchka* formerly *Isles du Frioul*.

16. A handshake for Tom Grossman after his finish in the trimaran *Cap 33*.

17. Specially designed to the limits of the Jester trophy class, *Spanie* was sailed into second place in the class and third overall by her Polish designer Kazimierz Jaworski (18).

19. Her chart table arrangement and the special sail locker in the prow are evidence of very thoughtful preparation for the race (20).

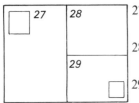

21	□	24
22	23	25	26

21. *The Third Turtle*, sailed by the Canadian Michael Birch, took an astounding second place overall and won the Jester trophy. He combined extraordinary seamanship with great dedication and the ability to put up with really spartan living conditions aboard (22 and 23).

24. *Pen Duick VI*, the unexpected victor. Thirty tons of yacht hurled along at more than ten knots in a heavy sea.

25 and 26. Eric Tabarly: he undertook all the duties of what would normally be a crew of 14.

□ 27	28
	29

27. Mike McMullen and *Three Cheers*. He and his boat disappeared without trace.

28. The press men crowd aboard even before *Pen Duick VI* come alongside the dock.

29. Tabarly gives his weary first impressions of the toughest race he has ever contested—even tougher than when he won before. An hour of glory.

□ 30

30. The 1976 winner and *Pen Duick VI*.

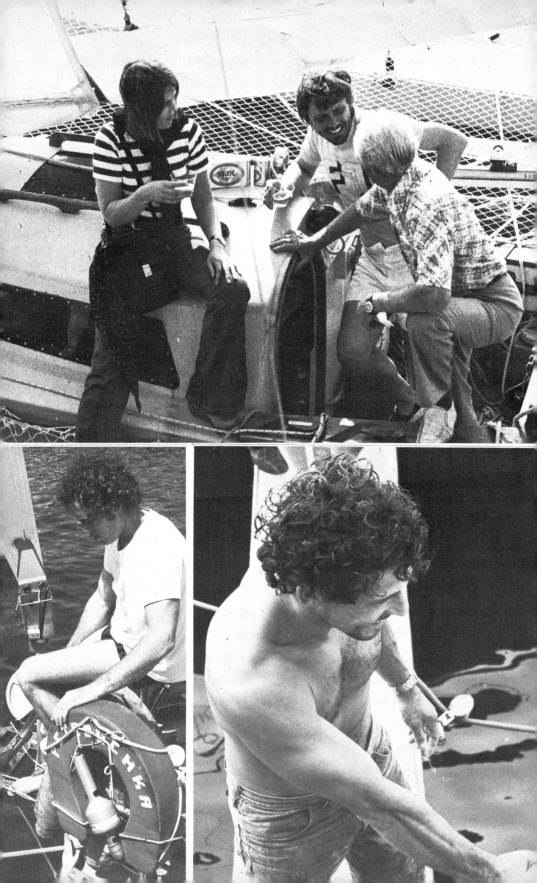

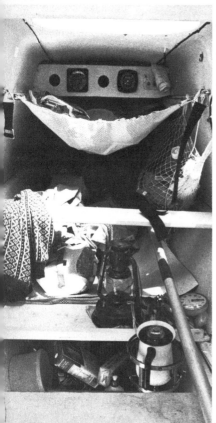

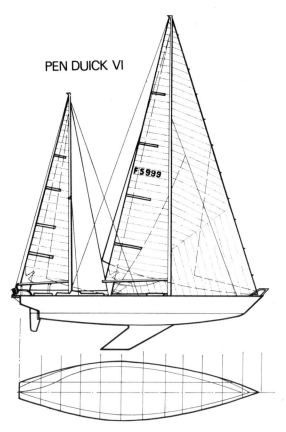

PEN DUICK VI

Boat plan
1976 Eric Tabarly—*Pen Duick VI*, winner in 23 days, 20 hrs 12 mns

Overall length: 73 feet
Construction: Aluminium hull with depleted uranium keel
Ketch rig
Designer: André Mauric
Builder: Arsenal of Brest

how this vast boat would behave in the water and how she would react to the waves, and that these fundamental questions had to be answered before work could begin on building. Research was therefore undertaken in a test-tank in Paris. The problem was not to decide whether one hull shape was better than another, but rather to check that the design itself was sound.

At this stage the Société Française d'Etudes et de Réalisations de Machines et d'Outillages (Sofermo) came into the picture. This subsidiary of Renault was responsible, among other things, for developing the Unisurf process for the mathematical definition of surfaces. This comprises geometrical analysis of any sort of form into elementary facets, working from the plans. These facets, which have a simple mathematical form, are defined by co-ordinates placed in the memory of a computer. This computer performs the necessary calculations and simultaneously controls an automatic drafting machine and another machine which cuts the model out in soft materials. From the definitions of surfaces stored in the computer's memory plans of components may be drawn and projections, sections, perspective drawings and three-dimensional models may be produced as well. From this data the model of Alain Colas' boat was created for tank-testing. Sofermo built the model from Michel Bigoin's drawings, to one twentieth scale, giving it a length of $11\frac{1}{2}$ feet. The centres of gravity and of buoyancy were scrupulously set in exactly the same places in the model weighing 78 pounds as they would be in the full-sized boat. The model behaved perfectly in still water and then artificial waves were created to reproduce the type of seas the real boat would be likely to encounter. The passage of the hull through the water was filmed and when the film was projected in slow motion the movement of the boat was clearly discernible. These tests proved successful and only slight modifications had to be made to the full-sized boat.

When tank-testing had been completed, several days' experiments on the rigging were undertaken in the wind-tunnel belonging to the Office National d'Etudes et des Recherches Aérospatiales. A model 23 feet long was constructed with an arbitrary heel of 12 degrees. The sail area amounted to 172 square feet, taking the three sails — mainsail, boomed staysail and genoa — together on each mast. In fact 'the search for the best compromise between the results of the wind-tunnel tests, real conditions and my physical condition,' Alain Colas admitted, 'led me to do away with the genoas altogether and just keep the mainsails, and to substitute boomed jibs for the staysails.' This decision meant that the sail area was close on 11,000 square feet.

The tunnel could simulate winds of any speed between 20 and 56 kilometres per hour as required. Although the actual results remained a closely guarded secret, both Michel Bigoin and Alain Colas agreed that these few days in the wind-tunnel were the equivalent of a whole season's sailing. The results obtained were not, of course, an exact pattern of the actual behaviour of the full-sized boat. Nevertheless they did enable some tests to be carried out far more simply, when you consider what the full size of the boat was in comparison with that of the model. The experiments proved that the sails set on each mast did not interact unfavourably, and provided interesting sidelights on the stability of the rigging in winds of differing speeds and direction. Thanks to a computer fitted below the hull, the strength of wind-pressure could be recorded from any pre-determined angle. Although the wind-tunnel did not answer all the questions at least it made a number of useful suggestions which led the designer to suppose that the sail-plan which he had evolved would behave correctly.

The hull had been tank-tested and the rigging had gone through the wind-tunnel without the need for radical modification. It was now up to the yards in Toulon to mobilise their craftsmanship and skill to successfully complete the building stage.

During the many months of his convalescence, Alain Colas devoted the best of his thought and energy to pondering on his steel monster. On 28 November 1975, he was able for the first time to visit the Toulon Naval Dockyard, where *Club Méditerranée* was being built. Seventy shipwrights were putting in a fifty-seven-hour week on this mammoth. You need a special team to successfully construct a 250-tonner, but the Dockyard knew all the latest methods for building large steel vessels and Colas' worries were considerably lessened because of this. The boat had been designed to be built in sixteen sections and they gradually took shape from drawing the full-sized templates to actual assembly. Overhead cranes set the sections side by side and then they were welded together. The boat was assembled upside-down to facilitate the work, so that she would have to be launched keel upwards, too.

The launch took place on 15 February 1976. The boat was slowly eased down the slipway to the water, and then gently shoved off. Still keel uppermost she was towed into the Vauban Dock in the port of Toulon. She looked peculiarly like a submarine with her keel instead of a conning-tower as she floated in the middle of a fleet of yachts. Moored alongside the dock, she was slowly eased over to an angle of about twenty degrees with the help of compressed air cylinders and a system of pulleys and hawsers which ensured that she tipped in the right direction. When the time came she went over without a hitch, carried by the 80-ton weight of her ballast and in a sheet of foam her keel hit the water. The monster floated perfectly on her lines and the first part of the operation had been successfully performed. The second part now had to be accomplished in a race against the clock, which was to complete fitting out and sail the qualifying 500 miles before 5 April.

From then on there was considerable British concern, and particularly on the part of the Race Committee of the Royal Western Yacht Club, for safety precautions in the forthcoming race. They were concerned, and rightly so, by the problems which would arise when one lone sailor brought a 236-foot yacht into Millbay Dock at Plymouth already filled with the other 120-plus competing yachts and the thousands of boats which followed the start. Some were disturbed at the thought of the first few days of the race sailed through the busy Channel shipping lanes, and they had visions of the 250-ton monster running down a yacht, a fishing-boat or even a cargo ship. The organisers decided to make quite certain the boat was manageable by insisting that Colas should sail 1500 miles singlehanded in the North Atlantic before 15 May ... rather like asking him to sail half a Singlehanded Race. On the other hand they did permit him to complete his qualifying 500 miles before 5 April with a crew. Now, the rules stipulated that nobody who has previously completed the Singlehanded Race need qualify personally, but his boat must do 500 miles with a solo skipper aboard, even if it is someone else. But this was not applied to Colas. The fears of the Committee when faced by a boat like this are understandable. On her qualifying sail off Toulon, *Club Méditerranée* occasionally reached the speed of 18 knots and maintained 10 knots for some hours.

Even while the yacht was being worked up for the race the whole basis for such a gigantic undertaking may be questioned. Should a race of this sort monopolise so much time and trouble? As early as 1972 Colonel Hasler had spoken out against the bold thinking behind *Vendredi 13*. As far as he was concerned the boat would not win and he hoped it would not, because, although it stood for a most attractive experiment, it was an experiment in totally the wrong direction. Admittedly, when the Colonel had inaugurated the race in 1960 to promote fresh ideas, he could never have foreseen that a 250-ton yacht would be among the starters one day. It is legitimate, too, to ask whether *Club Méditerranée* was such an original idea, and she certainly did not belong to that category of sailing improvement which Colonel Hasler had had in mind 16 years before.

The 1964 winner took a very severe line on this very point. In February 1976, Eric Tabarly remarked:

Alain Colas is going to have his big 236-foot mono-hull, although at this moment in time nobody knows if he will be able to race her in person. I wish him a speedy recovery, but I don't think he will start unless he is one hundred per cent fit. He owes this to the other competitors. If he is beaten, there should be no 'ifs' and 'buts' to take away from the winner's achievement. His boat adds nothing new to naval architecture. It is quite uninspired, being merely an enlarged version of *Vendredi 13* with all her defects as well, multiplied by two. It is even more under-powered than *Vendredi 13* was, and this presupposes that she will sail poorly in light and moderate winds. A boat rigged with eight sails set one behind the other cannot sail into the wind at the right angle, and this weakness against the wind threatens to be particularly awkward in the Singlehanded Race which generally enjoys westerly winds for most of the time. Nor do I believe that she will be very fast even when she has a crew. Although her rig may not be geared to speed, it is very well adapted for singlehanded sailing. If the deck plan and the arrangement of the running rigging have been well thought-out, there should be no difficulty in handling her. But I shall be surprised if *Club Méditerranée* comes in ahead of *Grand Large* and *Great Britain III.*

In the face of such criticism, Alain Colas was forced to go for victory. His boat's maiden voyage took place on 21 March, but there was little wind and three of the four jibs were missing so that little idea of the schooner's potential could be assessed. Nevertheless it could still be argued that she would be unhappy in light winds and that she needed plenty of wind in which to show her paces.

Gradually Colas overcame all obstacles as he proceeded towards his goal. During the weekend of 28 March he sailed his qualifying 500 miles in the Mediterranean with plenty of other people aboard. More fitting out followed and then he set off for the Atlantic.

At 10 am on Thursday, 12 May, the Le Havre pilot came aboard *Club Méditerranée* to guide her into harbour. In seven days singlehanded sailing she had covered 1500 miles and maintained an average of 9 knots. All had gone satisfactorily, and Colas had been able to keep her under full sail except for a short period when a halyard parted and a sail came down. However, he managed to set it again, but it was an omen of things to come. On stepping ashore he announced:

I am amazed by the qualities of the boat, and now I have her well in hand. In six and a half days I covered half the distance of the Singlehanded Race, and I think I shall win my bet that I shall cross in eighteen days, particularly as I was not pushing the boat to her limits . . . I've reassured the British [he ended with a broad grin], now I'm going to worry them!

A year earlier nobody could have foreseen that he would make Plymouth. Sheer guts and a willingness to take risks had brought him step-by-step towards the goal which he had set himself no matter how he was to reach it. When a newsman asked him about the speed of the boat, he answered: 'She has been designed to maintain a steady average speed rather than to have the capacity to make sudden spurts. She will have to keep up an average of between 8 and 9 knots on her ocean passage.'

Besides the fact that she constituted a source of danger for other boats in busy shipping lanes, Alain Colas also 'worried' the British by showing that *Club Méditerranée* was a fast sailer during the 1500 miles which he had completed singlehanded, however, the real cause of worry was far deeper and more serious. The whole spirit of the race had been called into question. By building a boat 236 feet long and worth the best part of a million pounds some thought Colas had broken the moral contract binding him to the rules. But as far as Colas was concerned, the sky was the limit since the object of the race as a sporting event was 'to encourage the development of boats, their rigging and of all technical aspects of crossing the Atlantic Ocean singlehanded under sail.'

The British mistake was to delay until too late their reactions to the deliberate challenge to them of the entry of the monster into the race. Perhaps they did not really believe that she would actually compete.

In Plymouth at the beginning of June people suddenly began to realise just how vast the whole undertaking was. Some were overwhelmed at the thought of one man being able to handle such a boat, and praised his courage. Others could not understand how anything so gigantic could have been built. What was so magic about 236 feet? Did it really have to be so long to win? Hadn't he bitten off more than he could chew? What was he thinking of? Surely, it was just a matter of money?

For the first time in the history of the race one of the entrants could not get into the dock because of her size. Beside her *Vendredi 13* looked very small indeed!

Following the requirement of a special 1500 miles qualifying cruise, the Royal Western again upset Colas. On 1 June in accordance with Rule 26 which stipulates that alterations of the rules may be made up to time of starting, Commander Lloyd Forster, Sailing Secretary to the RWYC signed an amendment which was distributed to all competitors. It stated that 'in addition to the navigational aids prohibited under Rule 23 (b), use of any navigational system based on space satellites was against the spirit of the race and was consequently prohibited.' The club's reasoning was that hyperbolic navigation aids were banned for all competitors. It could hardly allow one boat to use special gear which gave the skipper even more help than a hyperbolic position fixer.

Very obviously this decision had not been directed against a boat like *Jester*. Colas was the only competitor with equipment to fix his position by space satellite, fitted by the CSEE. 'I have called in the Sylostat,' Alain Colas had announced, 'because it enables me to know precisely and exactly where I am, whatever the weather.' The Doppler factor and the data transmitted by the six space satellites in the Transit system enabled the instrument automatically to calculate the position of the boat. The world-wide coverage provided by the satellites allowed a precise fix to be obtained at least every two hours, and, since he knew the speed and course of the boat, he could work out his position in the meantime by dead reckoning.

It requires little thought to see how useful such an instrument must be in a race of this nature, in which the last 500 miles — and in particular the landfall and the finish — are usually made in foggy weather. The race rules prohibit the use of hyperbolic systems of position fixing and it was at this point that confusion arose. Colas only fitted the Sylostat after informing the Race Committee that it used the Doppler factor, but

Colonel Odling-Smee later denied that the Committee had been so informed.

One has to remember here that the committee draws up the rules of each race fully three and a half years before the event. It is easily possible for some new piece of technology to outdate those rules during that period. Hence the need for a special rule which gives the committee freedom to publish late amendments — even if they do seem to be aimed specifically at one competitor.

Leading up to the 1976 race, the Royal Western Yacht Club had several meetings with Alain Colas at which their concern about the size of his huge boat was discussed. He was told well before the boat was launched that the entry would be refused, but managed to convert a previously hostile committee. He also asked for a special dispensation to use radar and other equipment banned by the rules, but this was not allowed since it would give him an unfair advantage. At that stage the satellite navigation system was not mentioned.

Then, after Colas suffered his accident, the committee reconsidered their earlier dispensation and decided that the entry would again have to be refused. Again Colas came to Britain to plead his case. And again the committee, impressed by the man's courage, determination, and remarkable recovery, agreed that he could enter the big schooner, but only if he agreed to sail the special 1500 mile singlehanded cruise.

Finally, when *Club Méditerranée* arrived at Plymouth and the professional adviser used by the Royal Western went aboard to seal off the banned gear, Colas vehemently disputed his authority over certain pieces of equipment — particularly the Sylostat. That was when the special amendment was promulgated.

The facts of this case illustrate perfectly the way in which the British applied the rule that the competitor should at all times act in the 'spirit of the race'. It is obvious that if you can reach Newport without touching your sextant and without having to use dead reckoning you take away a great deal of skill in the race and it would enormously reduce the qualities of seamanship if this were the only way in which a competitor could obtain a fix. Perhaps Colas considered it as 'encouraging all technical aspects of crossing the ocean singlehanded under sail'. The divergence of views as to what constituted the spirit of the race, when the race itself developed so far and so fast, should have been foreseen. The solution which left every competitor a relatively free hand provided that he acted in the spirit of the race was both honourable and praiseworthy when competitors pursued the same overall objective. But the number of skippers involved and the sophistication of their equipment combined to complicate the issue.

By 1976 the Singlehanded Race had almost become part of the scene. For some years, people had grown used to hearing of yachts handled by the lone sailor and for this reason there was not the same atmosphere surrounding the one hundred and twenty-five yachts assembled in Millbay Dock as there had been in the earlier Singlehanded Races when it had seemed unusual if not rash for one man to venture alone on the North Atlantic. And yet it was the sheer numbers of competing boats and above all their diversity which had made the event so renowned.

Once again Plymouth was the centre of frantic activity. Those who were early wandered round anxious not to miss anything that was going on. In the dock, the competitors went about their last minute preparations, taking advantage of the fact that they were able to enjoy the sunshine and to work on their boats snug in harbour. You need to have sailed the North Atlantic to visualise the conditions which they would meet in a few days' time. By the look of some of the boats it was hard to believe they were going anywhere.

After the safety inspection, some of the competitors left the dock to make final adjustments to the rigging. In the inner harbour Michael Kane's splendid trimaran had her spinnaker hoisted and *Pen Duick VI* sent up her own to make sure for the last time that the 'sock' system employed worked properly. This was a sort of sheath which enclosed the 'chute and folded it up like an accordion at the masthead with a pulley to release it. To take in the spinnaker, you let go the guy and hauled on the other halyard to release the sheath and trap the sail. However, *Pen Duick's* main concern was her self-steering gear. It had been fitted, all right, but within days of the start it was still without an apparatus to recharge its batteries. Now, as the rules specified that it must possess an independent power supply, the original idea had been to equip the boat with a water-driven generator. However, tests had proved inconclusive and delayed completion of a different type which was in the end assembled in the naval dockyard at Brest and fitted to the boat the very evening before the start. In addition to this equipment, *Pen Duick* had solar panels fitted to the deckhouse to act as a supplementary power supply.

Apart from the items of equipment essential for singlehanded sailing, *Pen Duick* had undergone very few modifications. The coffee-grinder winch had been given a fourth gear and a genoa had been specially made with reefpoints, so that fewer changes had to be made. Tabarly had also constructed a sail enclosure system which could be raised by a halyard and secured in three places to the deck to simplify lowering headsails, preventing them from going overboard in strong winds.

Very early on the morning of 5 June, Alain Colas cast off his moorings and took his monster into the Sound. A south-westerly was blowing at 10 knots. The crew who were to remain aboard until the last moment were busy and the sails were set one after another. The start was at noon and thirty minutes before the gun, the engine was switched off and sealed, and the big boat moved slowly close inshore under sail.

The escorting boats were like a swarm of a thousand flies, buzzing hither and thither across the outer harbour. It was best not to think what things would have been like if there had been a 35 knot wind blowing. People had wondered if Colas would anchor before the start, but he had made up his mind that what little wind there was allowed him to remain under way and he chose to be free to move.

ITT Oceanic had anchored some distance from the starting line with *Kriter III* moored alongside. Once their preparations were complete, Fauconnier cast Terlain off, the latter standing away under his mainsail. Then Fauconnier raised anchor and got under way with his three boomed jibs set.

Pen Duick VI with all sail set, including her big genoa, sailed calmly round waiting for the start.

Spirit of America came sailing close-hauled down to the end of the Sound under her mainsail — painted with the Stars-and-Stripes — and a huge well-cut genoa as well.

Noon, and the officials had cleared the starting line as best they could. Alain Colas made a superbly calculated start gently steering his boat on the starboard tack to give her a clear run. The featherlight American boat shot away, while Fauconnier passed astern drawing inshore on the starboard tack, as *Pen Duick* had done a few minutes before, having crossed a few yards ahead of the giant. The *Pen Duick* class were away.

It had all happened almost in slow motion, but the strain on the skippers could be guessed as they strove to clear the breakwater safely, avoiding the spectator boats, crossing one another's wake and keeping a firm eye on the feeble breeze for the opportunity to set out into the open sea. Sensibly Colas remained on starboard, waiting until he was far enough out to put the helm over. Fauconnier had come close inshore to avoid the current which ran from west to east but he was finding it hard to make progress. In such light weather conditions Terlain was also finding it slow work and he was busy trying to get the right set to his sails. Tabarly, meanwhile, had managed to clear the headland with ease and on the way out to the Scillies, he was as happy as a sandboy. By five o'clock he was pretty well ahead, with *Spirit of America* coming up on the starboard tack several miles behind him. *Three Cheers* was with them too, although she had started half-an-hour later, and McMullen's trimaran was well placed in the Gipsy Moth class. To windward were two other Gypsy Moth class boats — *Gauloises* was striding splendidly along, with *Bestevaer* a few miles behind her.

For a time the entire fleet was muddled up with the Jester class boats — the last class to start came up to join the others. The four *Frioul 38* boats were well placed as was the little trimaran *FT* and the lovely *Ackel France*. However, *Pen Duick VI* was, expectedly, the first boat to be seen from Lizard Point at sunset, leaving behind her the massive pack of a hundred and twenty-four other competitors.

With her sail fanned out to catch what little breeze there was, *Jester's* dark green hull bobbed gently on the calm sea. Glass in hand, Michael Richey sat back and enjoyed the first few hours of his escape to the high seas. Both were old hands — this was *Jester's* fifth Singlehanded Race and the third for her present skipper.

Far away by now to windward *Club Méditerranée* sailed towards the open Atlantic, driven by the eight sails set above her 236-foot decks. So many people had banked their hopes, their friendship or their money upon the 1972 winner, Alain Colas, that the one thing above all else for him was to race his massive boat with every ounce of skill and will power which he possessed. There was only one possible place for him: first place. The last round of the battle, which had begun years before, was undoubtedly going to be the toughest. It would have to be won in as near eighteen days as he could manage on the toughest route of all — the Great Circle.

As the skippers got ready for their first night on watch, in an area thick with cargo ships and fishing-boats, there was no question of their snatching more than the odd hour's sleep. Now was the time when the major decision as to choice of route became apparent. Those who had determined upon the northern track would pass close to the Scillies before heading into the Irish Sea, while the others, the small and the ultra-light boats, would head south-west for lower latitudes, reaching the area of following winds in just over a week. They made for the open sea without yet realising that they were going to take part in the toughest Singlehanded Race ever to be held.

In fact, in this fifth race the bad weather soon showed itself, and wind and sea rapidly began to rise. The south-west wind of the start veered to west and then swung back to south-west soon increasing to gale force. Five deep depressions swept one behind the other across the Atlantic. Generally the wind veers north-east between each bout of bad weather, allowing boats to tack on to starboard, the tack which took them towards their goal. It was to be different this time. The strong south-westerly blowing a few days after the start forced competitors to remain on the port tack, which explains why so few of them took the middle track and so many of them were driven willy-nilly towards the high latitudes and the true line of the Great Circle route.

Statistics show that the race is a matter of sailing close-hauled in a stiff breeze, and the weather during that first fortnight in June only went to confirm them. Between the fourth and the eleventh, competitors had to contend with five depressions in a row which generated winds averaging Force 8. However, the major factor was the two successive great gales, between the eleventh and the fourtenth in the first of which the wind gusted to Force 9 and in the second to Force 11. The competitors had in fact been caught in a disturbance caused by a movement of the Polar Front. The sharp contrast in temperature between the masses of cold air to the north and the warm air over Newfoundland and Europe had sent the depressions moving in a mean line which passed through the track of the race.

When you study a situation like this, you realise better than ever how this race has to be a matter of an indestructible boat and of a skipper skilled to the utmost in her handling. The 1968 race had been affected by a deep depression; in 1972 the weather had been kinder. Those who drew over-hasty conclusions from the latter, were to pay most cruelly for them in 1976. The singlehander must be able to maintain the upper hand day after day, resolutely, cold-bloodedly and courageously, while retaining a degree of flexibility to match the conditions prevailing at the time. He needs to be stubborn enough to maintain the upper hand by sheer physical strength in times of crisis, but not so pigheaded that he cannot bow before the power unleashed by the elements to save his boat and to remain in a state to handle her. The solution of the problem lies in discovering the proper balance, so that you can stick it right to the finish.

The glass had been going down steadily since the evening of the start and three days later, on 8 June, the wind increased to 40 knots, reaching 50 knots during the night and 60 in the early hours of the following day. In conditions like this plenty of boats could no longer continue under way and were forced to heave to in mountainous seas with waves breaking everywhere across the surface of the water.

From the start *Club Méditerranée* had fallen into her racing rhythm. Alain Colas made regular live broadcasts on Radio Europe No 1. He had already had trouble with halyards parting. The boat herself was comfortable enough in this sea, but although the rigging had been well planned it did suffer in these weather conditions and it is easy to imagine the sheer physical effort required of the skipper to control and reset an obstinate sail. The full and formidable sailing potential of the giant boat could not be realised in weather like this, during which neither the rigging nor the skipper's skill could bring the monster to heel.

On the morning of 9 June a container-ship, the *Atlantic Cognac*, crossed her track and observed that the foremast jib was trailing along the side of the hull and that the aftermast jib was on deck. The crew watched the four master, thinking that she was in for some dirty weather further west where they had steamed through winds of between 40 and 60 knots and waves 25 and 30 feet high!

On 8 June, Colas was in the same area as Tabarly. On the ninth they were still on the same longitude, but *Pen Duick* was nearly 150 miles further north.

Then Tabarly discovered that his self-steering gear was out of action. Exhausted by the last few hours he had spent on deck and remembering the trouble a similar failure had caused him in 1964, for a moment he lost confidence in his ability to reach Newport. It was then that he made up his mind, like a wise man and experienced seaman, and took the sensible decision for which he was to blame himself a few days later as a sign of weakness. As he wrote in his log:

Even if I have to go on, it will not be along the northern track. The southern route seems to me the only possible one. To get more sunshine so that the solar panels would be able to give full power and make it possible for me to use the self-steering gear occasionally, I put the helm over and with the foresail laid aback we ran at an angle of 60° to the wind at between 5 and 6 knots in a south-easterly direction. I had as good as retired from the race, but before I came to a final decision, I wanted to get some sleep . . . It was late by the time I surfaced on the ninth. Thoroughly rested, I saw matters in a different light and there was no question now of retiring. I was furious with myself for all the way I had lost to the east.

Colas had got clean away and having occasionally been able to average 12 knots, on 10 June he was 250 miles ahead of Tabarly.

By now there had been plenty of unfortunate retirements. Guy Cornou was injured and had turned back. Linski's boat sprang a leak and he put into Brest. Dominique Berthier was run down but her boat managed to limp to within a few miles of Ushant, where she was picked up by a trawler. *Toria* caught fire and sank, her skipper Tony Bullimore being picked up by the tanker *Ocean Chemist*. André de Jong's *Aquarius* retired after the self-steering gear broke down and Kees Roemer's *Bollemaat* put back to Plymouth with generator trouble. The Welshman Hywel Price had to pull out his yacht *McArthur* because of rudder troubles, and Edoardo Guzzetti, the Italian veteran of the 1972 race, also had to give up because his self-steering had broken. The Englishman Mike Best, sailing the trimaran *Croda Way*, had seen his mainsail ripped apart by the gale but was pushing on as best he could. Every day the Committee of the Royal Western Yacht Club announced fresh retirements due to the continuing bad weather. Finally, Joël Charpentier, whose big ketch *Wild Rocket* was in the *Pen Duick* class, was forced back to Brest because of damage to the rudder and sails. He was one of the last to turn back before the storm redoubled its violence. Around 14 June the weather reached its worst, and a fresh wave of accidents swelled the already long list of retirements.

Serious concern arose on shore as each weather forecast for the North Atlantic was worse than the one before and as messages began to come in from competitors. How many of them would manage to come through?

Tirelessly, Alain Colas continued to keep the entire French nation informed of his progress, and his listeners thought that his victory was a foregone conclusion. However, the troubles he was meeting made one or two of them change their minds. By 14 June nine halyards had parted and he could no longer carry canvas on his foremast, and for two days his progress had been virtually halted. It became obvious that the choice of such a boat to sail the North Atlantic singlehanded had been very much of a gamble. Had the winds remained under 35 knots he would have won a sweeping victory. With Force 10 winds, the sailing qualities of his boat were less convincing. It is one thing to get your crew to set the sails at the start, but quite another to get through storms unscathed, with all the singlehanded seamanship and sail changing that this implies. 'It's blowing very, very hard, there's a very, very big sea running, and things are pretty tough,' Colas told listeners to Radio Europe No 1, on 14 June. 'Every now and then real walls of water come crashing down on the boat.'

Not a sight or a sound of *Pen Duick* had been had since she passed Lizard Point at the head of the field. Was she still in the lead? Had she been forced to turn back? Knowing how bad the weather really was, by 14 June people were beginning to wonder where she had got to. While Alain Colas further to the north was clawing his way forward, Eric Tabarly was actually being driven back, the appalling weather conditions having forced him to heave to under bare poles. Once he had discovered that it was not the power supply which was defective but the self-steering gear which was out of action, Tabarly realised that the mizzen had become the all-important sail. By balancing the sail-plan, it would allow the boat to sail correctly on a reasonably steady course with tiller lashed. For the rest of the crossing this sail was to play a key role, becoming, in its way, a kind of secondary self-steering gear. To safeguard it Tabarly was forced to lay the boat ahull and run some 70 miles back to the north-east. For the second time *Pen Duick* had been unable to make headway to the west.

The situation was even more disturbing for the other competitors, and between 14–16 June three potential winners were forced to retire.

On the eleventh day of the race, when lying 36° W, 46° N, in other words some 1800 miles from Plymouth, Michael Kane decided to retire and return to his home port. The main reason for the withdrawal of the American trimaran was because none of the self-steering gear worked well enough to keep the boat on course in the storm. The boat had yawed and paid off so sharply that one of the struts linking the floats had snapped and *Spirit of America* began to make water. Like most of the other competitors, Kane had encountered winds of 60 knots and these had lasted for four solid days. Trouble with the mainsail had not helped, and feeling that victory was slipping from his grasp the skipper decided to withdraw. On his return to Plymouth, he claimed to have covered 300 miles on one day and 250 miles on several others! If only the weather had been kinder . . .

Both Fauconnier and Terlain were up with the leaders. They had encountered the same bad weather as the others, and although Terlain in *Kriter III* had felt considerable concern when he discovered that his self-steering gear had failed, in the end his hopes had risen once more when he found he could carry on somehow. He had not come through the foul weather at all badly and had even been able to get some sleep when hove to, the big catamaran behaving very well. He had come through several days of bad weather and his hopes were really beginning to rise when an irreparable accident doomed his boat to destruction. The forward crossbeam joining the two floats began to break up and soon the pressures on the hulls caused the after beam to suffer the same fate. Powerless, Terlain watched the multi-hull go to pieces under his feet. To carry on was out of the question, what time was left to him would have to be used to salvage as much gear as possible before she went down.

Meanwhile fate or ill-luck ordained that a few hundred miles away, Yvon Fauconnier should lose control of his huge 128-foot schooner. This is the story in his own words.

The accident happened when I was trying to lower the centre jib. All was going splendidly on board and I was on top of the world. I was even beginning to think that old *Vendredi* and I were going to be able to win the race, when at the start the thought had never crossed my mind. I had been driving hard for a couple of days, but as the wind was freshening I had lowered the fore and aft sails and securely furled them. It was blowing 50 knots by this time. My heart sang. Then the wind increased. The boat was running at 9 knots close-hauled under the centre jib. I thought the whole lot would go if the wind went on increasing. The seas were enormous and I had never seen anything like them . . . steep waves, 15 to 20 feet high coming at me from all directions. I put on my lifeline and came up on deck. It was splendid and really very impressive. We were doing a tremendous speed — 9 knots in a sea like that really was fast. I took hold of the handle of the winch and put all my weight on the brake. The handle spun free, smashed the metal buckle of my lifeline and beat a whole series of smashing blows on my arm and thigh. For a moment I was in a tricky situation, but I had the sense to hang on, because my lifeline was useless. Then I crawled astern, mad with anger. And there I sat completely powerless, while the sail blew itself to tatters, followed soon afterwards by the fore jib which broke free of its lashings and dangled pitifully over the side. The stern sail was the only one to remain furled. I sat stunned in the stern, utterly powerless when faced by a disaster as sudden as it was unexpected. The very heavy seas now became positively mountainous. In a state of utter chaos she broached, and I could not get her head to the wind. My arm had swollen enormously as well. I got in touch with the radio-doctor at Saint-Lys. I was getting the feeling back to my fingers after the first few minutes, so perhaps the arm was not broken. And the wind was still rising. The seas began to get dangerously heavy. It only needed one outsize wave and the boat would go right over.

For Fauconnier, too, the race was over. In France a rescue operation was mounted and in the end the Russian tug which had picked up Terlain (leaving *Kriter* to be battered by the waves until she sank) came alongside *ITT* and passed her a tow. Terlain and Fauconnier were together again and managed to save *ITT*, which was brought into St John's, Newfoundland, under tow.

Pierre Fehlmann was forced to abandon *Gauloises* when she sprang a leak in the bows. Fehlmann's rescue was one of the most dramatic stories of the 1976 race. The lightly built sloop had been making very good time until the big storm of the fourteenth. Then the huge seas proved too much for the sail box built into the bows. They broke through the box and *Gauloises* started to take water rapidly. He sent out a radio emergency message which was picked up by the weather ship *Romeo* and passed on to Portishead radio in Britain.

The station alerted all shipping in the area and the massive container ship *Atlantic Conveyor* went to the Swiss sailor's aid. Captain O'Brien, master of the ship described the rescue later. 'I have never seen such a terrifying prospect in all my forty-seven years at sea,' he said. 'The weather was very bad with a storm of wind, Force 10. We were plugging straight into the teeth of the wind with just steerage way. I didn't think it would be possible to rescue him. Certainly there was no possibility of putting a boat into the water.

We got gangway nets and safety harnesses suspended over the starboard side of the ship and then Fehlmann behaved in a very intelligent way. He is certainly a courageous sailor.

It was about 3.30 in the morning and we got as close to him as we could. *Gauloises* had lost her mast by this time but Fehlmann used the hull of the yacht as a sail in that terrific wind and managed to steer her alongside. Although we had put some oil over the side we knew that he wouldn't be able to swim in that sea so he had to be right first time.

He just got close enough to be able to jump into the netting as he sailed past. And just as he jumped the ship rolled and he was pushed under the water. But the crew pulled up the nets and got him aboard. He got away with his wet suit and his passport and that's about all. The boat drifted away but she couldn't have stayed afloat more than a few minutes.

Another early casualty had been Val Howells, the only veteran from the very first race to enter again in 1976. He had started in a specially designed 38-footer called *Unibrass Brython,* with his son Philip in a similar yacht providing an intriguing father and son race-within-the-race. But Val damaged a leg in a fall and decided he would have to put into Kinsale in Ireland, there to give up.

Also down, but not out, was the Dutchman Gerry Dijkstra in his sloop *Bestevaer.* The shrouds on his mast had taken such a pounding in the gales that they had chafed holes in the mast and were failing to give it proper support. Dijkstra had to turn back, though he restarted later and still finished inside the race time limit.

That week also saw the sad withdrawal of *Jester* — the only time in five races that she failed to finish the course. Her retirement was certainly in the Hasler spirit of the early races. Her skipper Michael Richey sent the laconic message 'Decided to abandon in favour of Irish cruise. No damage. No incident.'

This wholesale slaughter made it increasingly plain that weather conditions had been extraordinarily severe, and the lack of news of *Pen Duick* began to be very worrying.

By 19 June ten of Alain Colas' twenty halyards had parted and he was carrying no sail forward of the wheelhouse. He therefore decided to put into Newfoundland for repairs. The decision was forced upon him by the fact that the last thousand miles he had to sail were by all accounts subject to very light winds. It was difficult to see how *Club Méditerranée* could sail through these sort of conditions with only her four stern sails. Colas had to yield to necessity. From now on you felt you were watching the death of a stricken monster, which had no chance of winning. Having crossed the North Atlantic in record time, the huge boat fell victim to its own size. The news caused a considerable stir. The invincible Colas, who had daily sung the praises of his boat, had been forced to admit defeat. This merely confirmed some experts in what they had been saying all along, but others were frankly bewildered. As far as the public at large was concerned, they simply did not know what to think. A vast amount of support had been won by the story of the great 236-foot boat skippered by the lone sailor who had overcome the pain and handicap of a serious accident. However, perhaps the man had had too much to say for himself, telling all and sundry how fast his boat was going and proclaiming that second place was wide open for anybody else to take. Although there was still no news of *Pen Duick* sympathy had undoubtedly shifted behind her, and Tabarly was about to become the hero.

On 18 June, when Colas had put in to Newfoundland the false news was broadcast that Tabarly had been sighted 150 miles south of Cape Race. (This later turned out to be incorrect). In a few days he would be in Newport, we thought. But a week later *Pen Duick* was still not home. The calculations made of Tabarly's average speed, and based on the 'sighting' of 18 June, simply did not make sense, and it soon came out that nobody had really seen Tabarly at all. The only time he had been sighted was when he had passed Lizard Point on the first day of the race!

When he was interviewed on his arrival, Alain Colas seemed convinced that the rumour of Tabarly being sighted had been put about deliberately.

> The fact that the news that Eric had apparently been sighted ahead of me [he said] was only given to the world a few hours after I had announced my intention of putting in makes me think, and will make me go on thinking for a long time... as far as I am concerned it seems to be a really sinister coincidence. It makes me draw certain very definite conclusions.

However, Colas needed nearly thirty hours to repair his boat and when he set sail once more from Newfoundland, Tabarly, whose position was still unknown, had in fact regained the lead which he had lost to the four master when the two gales had forced him to heave to.

On 22 June, they were both roughly on the same longitude, but the ketch was much further south. On the 25 they did not realise that they were within 75 miles of one another. The game was by no means over, but *Pen Duick* was showing how much more easily she handled in light winds by comparison with the big four-master, and in June 1976 light winds were markedly prevalent on that particular part of the course off Nova Scotia.

There had been talk of lowering the record in 1976 to eighteen days. At the time of the start, this had seemed within the bounds of possibility, given that both Colas' boat and Tabarly's were entered, and both men had been thinking in terms of a crossing of under twenty days. There was still no news of *Pen Duick* twenty-three days later, while *Club Méditerranée* was regularly reporting her position and was expected into Newport the following day. Many thought first place must be in Colas' grasp. While he was 30 miles from home, no other competitor had been spotted so close to the finish. The night before Colas was due into Newport, the notorious fog had closed in and no spotter plane had been able to take off. Newsmen, who had been keeping watch all round the clock, lost patience and, kept regularly posted on Alain Colas' progress, expected to greet him late in the morning of Tuesday, 29 June. For the first time in the history of the race, the winner would have to make his own landfall — which sheds a sidelight on the difficulties of the race that year. For the moment Tabarly, who was causing ever-increasing anxiety, was forgotten — the limelight was on the four master.

Then came the sensation as *Pen Duick* slipped like a ghost right into Newport Harbour at three o'clock in the morning, picking her way between the moorings under main and mizzen-sails. Tabarly seemed tired as he stood by the tiller in his oilskins, but a smile lit up his face, for he had just heard that nobody was ahead of him. His exhausting struggle had been rewarded in the end. It had been a fiercer struggle than any he had had to endure in all his time at sea and in weather such as he had never met before. After chasing victory with his crew over thousands of miles raced all round the world, these 3000 miles sailed singlehanded crowned the career of a boat dogged by misfortune. And what a reward it was!

Although the damage suffered by so many of the other competitors might have made one fear for the worst, *Pen Duick* was unscathed. Her foredeck was neat and clean; the headsails were stowed away in their bags below decks; there was not a single dirty plate in the galley; the chart table was in apple-pie order, and the mooring lines were ready coiled in the bows. The self-steering gear was the only vital piece of equipment on board which had been smashed, but the breakdown of numerous secondary items showed how very tough the going had been. For example, the wheel-chains had slackened, forcing the skipper to steer directly with the tiller. As far as the rigging was concerned, a single forestay had snapped, but some of the navigational equipment had not functioned well. The off-course alarm, for example, went out of action after the first few days, and this would have provided Tabarly with invaluable assistance when his self-steering gear was not working. The electronic instruments showing wind-speed and direction had broken down as well, but fortunately only a few days before the end of the race. The heating never worked and the generating equipment with the task of providing electricity for 'domestic' purposes did not last out the race. It may therefore be said that navigational aids and those things which make life at sea more comfortable, particularly during a singlehanded race in such tough conditions, virtually did not exist as far as Tabarly was concerned. The extraordinary qualities of the boat, and particularly her steadiness in holding a course without self-steering gear enabled Tabarly to finish the race, while his own matchless seamanship, tenacity of purpose and hardiness combined to bring him in to Newport first.

They enabled him to come virtually unscathed through five big storms, to continue under way no matter what it cost in the light and shifting winds of the last 500 miles of the course, to make his way past all obstacles in the fog at the finish, to pick up the Brenton Tower and enter Newport and find that he had won. 'Not bad,' was all he was to say having put every ounce of energy into his 23 day, 20 hour, and 12 minute passage westward. When interviewed by *The Observer* in Newport, his comment was: 'It is just a question of muscles.' But his English is even more monosyllabic than his French, and it came out 'mooskles'.

The French newspapers were delighted and *Le Figaro* said:

Two things in Tabarly's victory are worthy of our admiration — the dramatic way in which it happened and the lack of noise about it. *Pen Duick* disappeared from the moment she left Plymouth. From the beginning to the end of his exploit, it was as though Tabarly was not there ... He won at the very moment when the French Navy was about to launch a general search for him. We had thought he would win, instead it looked as if he was dead. We thought he was dead, and then heard he was the winner ...

Three mass-circulation weeklies had Tabarly's picture on their covers the Monday following his victory. On 30 June, the day after he crossed the finishing line in America, the crowd shouted his name down the Champs-Elysées in a demonstration organised by the radio network which had been backing Colas three weeks before.

At Newport the telegrams were flooding in. At first they came neatly sealed, but soon they were flowing hot off the Telex. The Post Office was overwhelmed by the congratulations in all shapes and sizes.

In the Singlehanded Race, the general public takes much less notice of the second boat home, yet *Club Méditerranée* was only 25 miles away when a victorious *Pen Duick* crossed the finishing line. In the final result there was only seven hours, twenty-three minutes between the two boats. It was a grievous disappointment for Alain Colas, thinking as he did that he had won. It was very small consolation that his record still stood. You cannot rewrite history, but it is perfectly true to say that if his halyards had not parted, there is every reason to suppose that his monster would have carried off the victory. The halyards seem to have parted because on the back of each of the sheaves was a small pendant placed there to bend the outer halyard. Thus the play in the mast caused the halyards to chafe until in the end slowly but surely they parted. Seen in this light, his defeat was very bad luck. A few more months of preparation would no doubt have removed this flaw but was it the only one? Alain Colas sailed an extraordinarily courageous race during which there were times when the gigantic boat that he himself had created took charge of him. It is easy to be wise after the event, but it does seem as if this fiendishly difficult race allows nothing to be left to chance. The price of lack of preparation is very high indeed.

Pen Duick IV won in 1972, having been forced to retire in 1968. That year Terlain lost by a very few hours — in an inadequately prepared boat. Having won once, Alain Colas ought to have known this. He never doubted for a single moment that he would win. The results of all this titanic effort, handicapped by his accident, were heartbreaking for him and he had great difficulty at Newport in swallowing his defeat.

> When I put into Newfoundland — and I was stuck there longer than I had planned because I could only get hold of one other person to work on the sails — I conceded Eric the victory which was mine by rights after all the effort I had put in across the North Atlantic.

And remember what he said when *Club Méditerranée* hit the water for the first time:

> A 236-foot sailing vessel is not designed out of the blue. It is the result of ocean crossings, of getting to know what navigating under sail really means, what the sea is all about and thinking out the best uses of modern technology. When her hull hit the water and she became a boat, it was as wonderful as sitting on the roof of the world.

He certainly had trouble in coming down to earth at the end of the race, and the ten per cent penalty (fifty-eight hours) which he incurred under Rule 22 (2) led him into a series of blistering accusations against the Race Committee. The rule lays down that when a boat comes into harbour and ties up at the quayside or moors on a buoy, other people are allowed on board. It also says that the yacht is allowed to be towed in and out of port for a maximum distance of two miles. The story of what happened in St Johns was very carefully put together by Colonel Odling-Smee, since it was clear at that time that Colas was very close to challenging for the outright victory. He discovered the replacement sails ordered by Colas — one of them from *Manuréva* — did not arrive in St Johns until just before the pilot went off duty. However the pilot agreed to take the yacht out and the sails were put aboard. Seven or eight crewmen went aboard too and the schooner was taken out to sea. The pilot returned to finish his tour of duty and another pilot then went out and picked up the crew members to bring them back to port.

By this time *Club Méditerranée* was some three miles off shore with all sails set. Colonel Odling-Smee described this as 'a gross breach of our rules and even if there had been no such rule it was clearly not singlehanded sailing. The proper course for the committee was to disqualify *Club Méditerranée*. However, Colas — in spite of all the difficulties he had had to face since his accident — had brought this great vessel safely across the ocean. It was truly an incredible feat of planning, seamanship and courage in adversity. In view of this the committee decided not to disqualify him but to impose a ten per cent penalty on his elapsed time.' This had the effect of demoting Colas from second to fifth place overall.

(Editor's note: In view of some of the French comments on the Royal Western's attitude towards the French contestants, it is enlightening to read the further comment of Colonel Odling-Smee. 'Many people consider that the committee should not have allowed Club Méditeranée *to enter in the first place. I am glad we did not take this view. Had it not been for his accident and had he carried out the trials he proposed, the trouble Colas had with his halyards would have been sorted out before the race and I believe he would surely have won.')*

Once the two giants were safely home to Newport, the race might have lost all remaining interest. However, twenty-five hours after *Pen Duick* crossed the line a minute trimaran designed by Dick Newick turned up in Newport. *The Third Turtle* looked as though she had just sailed across from the other side of the bay, but she really and truly had started from Plymouth on 5 June with her skipper, Michael Birch, a professional yacht-deliverer and, most surprising of all, her route had been more or less along the rhumb line. This amazing little craft, only 31 feet overall and displacing less than $1\frac{1}{2}$ tons, had put up an extraordinary performance, that of coming in third, or rather second when Colas had been penalised into fifth place. She was also a clear first in the *Jester* class and ahead of all the *Gypsy Moth* yachts. To do so she had survived all the foul weather, sometimes riding out the Force 9 winds. She belonged to the under 38-foot class, the smallest boats to be entered, and her designer, Dick Newick, had made his name in the yachting world in 1968 with *Cheers,* which so very nearly won the race on the southern track, and he had gone on to establish a worldwide reputation for his multi-hulls. With her Kevlar-reinforced struts and her canoe-shaped floats, *The Third Turtle* was as light as a cork. She hove to when she could no longer make headway, but when conditions permitted her to sail, she sailed to her full potential. Handling a seven-eighths jib — and a mainsail of the same area — seemed child's play except that sailing a dragonfly like that required seamanship of no common order.

The fourth home to Newport was yet another competitor in the Jester Trophy class, *Spaniel*, a traditional moulded wooden mono-hull sloop built by her owner and designer Kazimierz Jaworski with the help of a few friends, all naval architects from the Stettin Yacht Yard in Poland. She had been built the year before, specifically for the race. She displaced 5.2 tons and her length was calculated for her to qualify for the Jester class at 38 feet. Like all the competitors who chose the northern route, her skipper, Jaworski, took a course more or less along the Great Circle, to pass within 100 miles of Cape Race. He had encountered Force 11 winds which had forced him to heave to under bare poles. *Spaniel's* accommodation was worthy of an experienced seaman, as was the little enclosed cockpit which allowed the boat to be steered in safety. Despite all this, a wave well and truly smothered her and flooded her to fifteen inches above the cabin floor. Luckily, the boat had her pumps in working order! The stay for the furling genoa became badly worn and left *Spaniel* without foresails for a time. A second stay, slightly astern of the other, allowed the Pole to carry on in the race — and to keep sailing at a reasonable speed. Jaworski's splendid effort shows what proper race preparation really is, and every single thing on board reflected his eye for detail. *Spaniel's* twenty-five day passage along the hardest track provides incontrovertible evidence that a small mono-hull can weather the severest storms if she is properly designed.

Tom Grossman's *Cap 33* was the first boat home along the southern route. Although the winds on this track had sometimes reached Force 9, the weather had been far kinder than further north. Nonetheless it had been far worse than in any other year and not once did competitors who had chosen this route find the kindly trade winds for which they hoped. Prevailing winds had been almost uniformly west or south-west and therefore *Cap 33* put up a far slower time than when Jean-Marie Vidal had skippered her in 1972. The other surprising fact was that twenty of the twenty-six days at sea had been overcast. All this goes to show that in June 1976 the North Atlantic behaved in a very unusual way. Taking the westerly gales on the northern track into account, opinion was that the southern route would provide the winner — but it was not to be.

Petrouchka (ex-*Isles du Frioul*) took the Gipsy Moth Trophy by finishing sixth. Jean-Claude Parisis had deliberately chosen the Great Circle route. What is surprising is that on the eleventh day of the race his main halyard parted and he lost the use of his mainsail. For the last seventeen days he raced with a furling headsail, varying its area to suit the wind conditions. The only other damage recorded was to the underwater blade of the self-steering gear and this the Frenchman was able to repair while under way.

The first Briton home was David Palmer, who completed the race in twenty-seven days in his trimaran *FT*. He took the southern route, dropping right down to the forty-first parallel and giving the other top multi-hull designer, Derek Kelsall, a place in the first ten. Palmer encountered much the same wind conditions as Grossman and reached Newport on an afternoon of glorious sunshine as all the tall ships that had been in Newport after sailing in their own transatlantic race to celebrate the American bicentenary were heading for New York under full sail. Paradoxically, in this race the ones who suffered no damage and had no complaints all made splendid voyages. Like Birch, Palmer had no problems!

All those who managed to cross the Atlantic deserve respect and there should be a special pat on the back for Clare Francis and her 38-footer *Robertson's Golly*. She was the first woman home, shattering Marie-Claude Fauroux's time with a new record of twenty-nine days. Despite the bad weather conditions, she had succeeded in hitting her target of sailing into Newport on Sunday 4 July — the day of the Bicentennial celebrations. And all that despite having to lie a-hull for long periods with all sails down as the worst of the storms screeched and howled all around her. We soon discovered, when she arrived, that the tiny English girl had been very busy on her passage across the Atlantic. She had sent messages back to *The Daily Express* every other day, had made copious notes of her voyage for a book which appeared less than six months after she reached Newport, and she also managed to shoot a roll of ciné film each day — complete with sound commentary — which was later used by the BBC to form the bulk of its fifty-minute documentary programme on the Singlehanded Race.

And as if that were not enough, Clare also had her moments of high drama. The worst was when her self-steering gear was severely damaged and she had to make tremendous efforts to haul it inboard over the transom. She is only 5 feet 2 inches tall and weighs a mere 7½ stone, yet she lifted the heavy equipment inboard and managed to make makeshift repairs. When *Robertson's Golly* sailed into Newport, the gear was held together with a complicated cat's cradle of lashings — but it was still working.

Clare's other bad moment was when she came on deck to find that her yacht had just sailed between two massive icebergs. Her book, *Come Hell or High Water,* captures the worst moments of the crossing with graphic simplicity. Of one storm she wrote:

> The movements of the boat were severe. She would rush at a wave, leap off the top then crash down on to the other side, give a quick roll or flip, then rush at another. Sometimes she found nothing but air as she leapt off a crest and there would be a ghastly moment of silence before a terrible, juddering crash as the bows hit the water.
>
> So this was the great adventure, I thought, disconsolately. Gales that went on for ever, wet long johns, soggy food that was impossible to cook, damp books that fell apart in my hands and, worst of all, no one to complain to.

As the successful boats arrived ever more regularly in Newport, so the reports of casualties and withdrawals kept pace. Angus Primrose, designer of the boat he was sailing — *Demon Demo* — was completely inverted by the worst storm and had to fashion a makeshift jury rig on what was left of his mast in order to sail back to Plymouth. Richard Clifford was knocked down twice in his 26-footer *Shamaal II* and lost his main compass. He managed to finish the course and arrived in Newport having steered most of the way by a tiny orienteering compass just two inches in diameter.

John de Trafford sailed *Quest* over the line with her front crossbeams lashed together with a spinnaker pole and miles of rope. The heavy going had certainly put a severe strain on that big trimaran's construction.

Even Jock McLeod reported some troubles when he sailed his lugsail schooner *Ron Glas* across the line in forty-fifth place. A great believer in the lugsail rig (in fact he designs them) he had always been proud of the fact that he sailed his boat to Newport in the 1972 race without ever putting oilskins on. This time he had to break his routine. 'There was a snag in the halyard which I had to go up and sort out,' he said. 'Otherwise I was reefing and unreefing all the time from within the cockpit. It was not such an enjoyable passage as last time. I became very bored by the calms in the latter part of the crossing.'

But Jock had managed to make good progress with his colourful tapestry of *Ron Glas*. You certainly find a very wide variety of characters in the fleet of a Singlehanded Race.

Fifty days was the maximum allowed, competitors taking longer being omitted from the official list of finishers, and by 23.59 hours GMT on 25 July, seventy-three boats had reached Newport. Never before had a Singlehanded Race been so destructive, with nearly fifty boats retiring for various reasons. Some had sunk, others had been abandoned, but most of them had been able to put back to Europe or head off to the Azores.

However, for the first time there were two deaths to mourn. At 8 am on 30 June, SS *Nima* sighted *Galloping Gael* at 43° W by 47° 30' N. There was no one on board — Mike Flanagan had vanished. It is impossible to say what had happened, but it is likely that the unfortunate skipper was swept overboard by a wave. The second disappearance was that of Mike McMullen, who should have been among the first home to Newport, given the speed of his multi-hull, *Three Cheers*. He never arrived and no valid reason can be put forward to account for his disappearance since his boat was lost without trace. Possible theories are that either he was swept overboard, or else his trimaran capsized, or she broke up in mountainous seas, perhaps after a collision. Unfortunately risks like these are all part of the game.

No two Singlehanded Races are ever the same and the one in 1976 was the toughest to be held since the race began. There are some possible changes to the rules which could improve the event. In particular it would be far more exciting for all concerned if they could follow the progress of each individual boat. Yet there is no virtue in the solution which would make it compulsory for all boats to report their position daily. The French Centre National d'Etudes Spatiales had an answer when it suggested to the Race Committee that each of the boats should be fitted with one of its Argos-system transmitters. This would enable the Committee to know at all times the precise position of any one of the yachts taking part. Alain Colas had a similar system fitted to his boat in 1972. But, of course, transmitters cost money and that could be a deterrent.

Every difficulty which had been predicted before the start of each of the four previous races struck in 1976 — gales, fog, light winds, icebergs and cold.

Now a third family of sail-driven craft, differing from the multi-hulls, is about to see the light of day in the hydrofoil. Eric Tabarly has

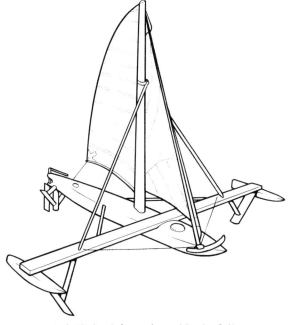

Eric Tabarly's projected hydrofoil.

collected a research team and is enthusiastic about the project which will write a fresh chapter in the history of singlehanded ocean sailing as an exciting new idea. Alain Gliksman is also thinking of a hydrofoil boat, and Dick Newick has some ideas of his own.

Once again in 1980 singlehanders are going to try to beat the record across the North Atlantic despite the limitation which prohibits boats over 56 feet long. In the age of Concorde the stakes seem pitifully small and yet they play their part in tempering a race of men ever seeking to discover themselves and their limitations. The Battle of the Atlantic is by no means over.

RESULTS OF 1976 SINGLEHANDED RACE

START: 5 JUNE

Order of Arrival	Boat	Class	M/G/T	Skipper	Elapsed time	Class placing
1	PEN DUICK VI	P	M	E. Tabarly	23 20 12	1
2	CLUB MÉDITERRANÉE	P	M	A. Colas	26 13 36*	3
3	THIRD TURTLE	J	T	M. Birch	24 20 39	1
4	SPANIEL	J	M	K. Jaworski	24 23 40	2
5	CAP 33	P	T	T. Grossman	26 08 15	2
6	PETROUCHKA	G.M.	M	J. C. Parisis	27 00 55	1
7	FT	J	T	D. Palmer	27 07 45	3
8	FRIENDS	J	T	W. Greene	27 10 37	4
9	ARAUNA IV	G.M.	M	J. Timsit	27 15 32	2
10	OBJECTIF SUD 3	J	M	A. Gabbay	28 09 58	5
11	MOONESHINE	G.M.	M	F. Stokes	28 12 46	3
12	VENILIA	G.M.	M	C. Bianchi	28 00 15	4
13	ROBERTSON'S GOLLY	J	M	C. Francis	28 23 22*	6
14	TYFOON V	J	M	G. Versluys	29 21 12	7
15	QUEST	G.M.	T	J. de Trafford	30 07 30	5
16	PAWN OF NIEUWPOORT	J	M	Y. Anrys	30 15 34	8
17	NOVA	J	T	E. Riguedel	30 15 34	9
18	ACKEL FRANCE	J	M	G. Vaton	31 03 12	11
19	LORCA	J	M	D. Pierre	31 14 45	10
20	SIRTEC	G.M.	M	P. Dumas	31 23 09	6
21	OLD MOORE'S ALMANACK	G.M.	T	G. Hornet	32 02 06	8
22	TAHITI BILL	G.M.	C	W. Howell	32 05 19*	7
23	WILD RIVAL	J	M	G. Hales	32 13 48	12
24	PETIT BRETON	J	M	B. Pallard	32 19 57	13
25	DADZTOY II	J	M	F. Graf	32 20 55	14
26	CARINA	G.M.	M	E. Raab	33 01 22	9
27	ADHARA	J	M	R. Ryott	33 02 54	16
28	PIERRE	J	M	P. Riboulet	33 03 39	15
29	HELENE III	J	M	G. Bucking	33 08 41	18
30	SHAMAAL II	J	M	R. Clifford	33 12 51	17
31	WIND QUEST	G.M.	M	E. Everett Smith	34 08 44	10
32	PYTHEAS	J	M	B. Veenemans	34 10 10	19
33	AZULAO	J	T	N. Clifton	35 03 35	20
34	INNOVATOR OF MANA	J	M	J. Mansell	35 12 25	21
35	FROMSTOCK FILIUS	J	M	P. Howells	35 16 07	22
36	FREEMERLE	J	M	D. K. Clark	35 22 50	23
37	KOR KAROLI	J	M	G. Gieorgiev	36 01 50	24
38	PATRIARCHE	J	M	E. Oliveaux	36 05 14	25
39	JABULISIIWE	J	M	I. Radford	38 08 44	26
40	SWEDLADY	J	M	L. Walgren	36 11 10	27
41	CHICA BOBA	G.M.	M	E. Austoni	37 06 00	14
42	EVA	J	M	I. Castiglioni	37 10 20*	30
43	EVALOA	J	M	E. Labourgade	37 10 24	28
44	LILLIAM	J	M	C. Schrodt	37 21 25	29
45	RON GLAS	G.M.	M	J. McLeod	38 17 40	11
46	EDITH	J	T	R. Nugent	39 04 30	31
47	ACHILLES NEUF	J	M	C. Butler	39 06 02	32
48	CRISAN	G.M.	M	J. Guiu	39 08 15	12
49	NIKE	J	M	R. Konkolski	39 10 49	33
50	ENGLISH ROSE IV	J	M	J. Young	39 11 29	34

51	GALWAY BLAZER	G.M.	M	P. Crowther	39 12 57	13
52	CATAPHA	J	M	D. White	39 17 15	35
53	TULOA	J	M	H. G. Mitchell	41 11 59	36
54	CASTANUELA	J	M	E. Vidal Paz	42 10 10	37
55	WESTWARD	J	M	David Pyle	42 10 11	38
56	MIRANDA	G.M.	M	Z. Puchalski	42 13 14	15
57	AMITIÉ	J	M	W. Wanders	42 17 30	39
58	HESPERIA	J	M	H. Jukkema	42 21 18	40
59	ACHILLE	J	M	M. Bourgeois	43 08 41	42
60	TIKKA III	J	M	C. Di Majo	44 00 37	43
61	LADY ANNE OF ST DONATS	J	M	D. Sutcliffe	44 03 47	41
62	CAIPIRINHA	J	M	A. Preden	44 04 45	44
63	GOLDEN HARP	J	M	S. Woods	44 19 14	45
64	CASPER	J	M	M. Wills	44 21 05	46
65	LAURIC	J	M	R. Elliott	45 02 29	47
66	JANINA	J	M	H. Pottle	45 03 12	48
67	DRAGON	G.M.	M	M. Bourgeois	45 12 45	16
68	AIREDALE	J	M	D. S. Cowper	46 11 17	49
69	GALADRIEL OF LOTHLORIEN	J	M	N. Lang	48 03 10	50
70	SONGEUR	J	M	R. Kendal	49 05 40	51**
71	BESTEVAER	G.M.	M	G. Dijkstra	49 07 22	17
72	BYLGIA	G.M.	M	E. Kasemier	49 10 34	18
73	PRODIGAL	J	M	R. Lengyel	49 19 30	52

2 : 58 hrs
*Penalty times 13 : 2 hrs 30 min
22 : 24 hrs
42 : 2 hrs
** Restarted from Plymouth 30 June

P: 'Pen Duick Trophy' M: Mono-hull
J: 'Jester Trophy' C: Catamaran
G.M.: 'Gipsy-Moth Trophy' T: Trimaran

RETIREMENTS

Race No.	Skipper	Boat	M/T/C	Length	Class	Date	
134	Guy Cornou	Kervilor	M	33½'	J	8/6	*Skipper injured*
40	André De Jong	Aquarius	M	28'	J	9/6	*Self-steering gear damaged*
8	Kees Roemers	Bollemaat IV	M	45'	GM	10/6	*Battery trouble*
97	Hywel Price	MacArthur	M	35'	J	10/6	*Rudder-tab damaged*
113	Marc Linski	Objectif Sud 1	M	38'	J	10/6	*Self-steering gear damaged*
56	Edoardo Guzzetti	Namar 5	M	41'	GM	11/6	*Self-steering gear damaged*
148	Mike Richardson	Arctic Skua	M	31'	J	11/6	*Self-steering gear damaged*
41	A. M. Bullimore	Toria	T	42'	GM	12/6	*Caught fire and sank*
20	Jock Brazier	Flying Angel	M	63'	GM	12/6	*Power-supply to self-steering gear failed*
69	Pierre-Yves Charbonnier	Karate	M	32½'	J	12/6	*Skipper injured*
124	Dominique Berthier	Saint Milcent	M	37'	GM	12/6	*Run down and sank*
157	Joel Charpentier	Wild Rocket	M	63'	P	12/6	*Trouble with standing and running rigging*
49	John Christian	Ek Soeki	M	27'	J	12/6	*Skipper poisoned by water supply*
45	Jean Yves Terlain	Kriter III	C	70'	P	13/6	*Sank after failure of hull structure*
27	Mike Richey	Jester	M	26'	J	13/6	*Retired undamaged*
28	Val Howels	Unibrass Brython	M	38'	J	13/6	*Injured leg*
51	Pierre Fehlmann	Gauloises	M	57'	GM	14/6	*Boat abandoned after being dismasted and springing a leak*

136	Jean-Claude Montesinos	Keep Cap d'Adge	M	55'	GM	15/6	*Not known*
181	C. H. la Moing	Pronuptia	M	43'	GM	15/6	*Damage to sails*
93	Chris Smith	Tumult	M	22½'	J	15/6	*Sickness*
39	Yvon Fauconnier	ITT Oceanic	M	128'	P	15/6	*Arm injured by slipping winch handle*
122	C. S. W. Ward	Altergo	T	39'	GM	15/6	*Damaged tiller*
145	Paolo Mascheroni	Panda 31	M	31½'	J	15/6	*Not known*
170	Guy Brunet	Ironiguy	M	32'	J	16/6	*Damage to self-steering gear*
133	Mike Best	Croda Way	T	35'	GM	16/6	*Damaged float*
162	P. Szekely	Nyarlathotep	M	42'	GM	17/6	*Boat sinking*
193	Oscar Debra	Vanessa	M	43'	GM	18/6	*Returned to Plymouth*
22	Hans Joachim Schulte	Silke	M	25'	J	18/6	*Damage to self-steering gear causing leak*
104	Doi Malingri di Bagnolo	CS & RB Busnelli	M	60'	GM	19/6	*Shrouds parted following collision with unidentified vessel*
53	Christian le Merrer	Acteia II	M	36'	J	22/6	*Collision with Spanish fishing-boat*
76	Michael Kane	Spirit of America	T	62'	P	23/6	*Breakage in connecting strut*
151	Andrew Bray	Gillygaloo	M	32'	J	24/6	*Self-steering gear damaged by collision with whale*
153	Colin Drummond	Sleuth Hound	M	32'	J	24/6	*Rigging damaged*
186	Alain Marcel	Drakker III	M	38'	GM	25/6	*Self-steering gear damaged*
12	R. J. Ogle	Jade	M	51'	GM	26/6	*Failure of electronic instruments*
11	Heiko Krieger	Tinie II	M	36'	J	28/6	*Mast damaged*
101	Gérard Frigout	Pen-Ar-Bed	M	40'	GM	29/6	*Not known*
32	Ambrogio Fogar	Spirit of Surprise	C	25'	J	1/7	*Struts linking floats broken*
120	Angus Primrose	Demon Demo	M	33'	J	2/7	*Capsized and dismasted*
62	Paolo Sciarretta	Valitalia	M	45'	GM	2/7	*Not known*
160	Aline Marchand	Logo	M	38'	J	9/7	*Dismasted*
126	Patrick O'Donovan	Silmaril	T	31'	J	22/7	*Dismasted*
172	Johnathan Virden	Sharavoge	M	25'	J	29/7	*Put in to Bermuda*
15	Brian Start	True North	M	38'	J	2/8	*Put in to Halifax*

Late finishers (after midnight 25 July):

84	Jean Ropert	Bigouden Brise	M	27½'	J		
158	F. Sloan	Ballyclaire	M	33½'	J		

● *Lost:*

99	Mike McMullen	Three Cheers	T	46'	GM		*Lost without trace*
6	Mike Flanagan	Galloping Gael	M	38'	J		*Boat found abandoned with nobody on board 1/7*

BIBLIOGRAPHY

Les Solitaires de l'Atlantique
Alain Gliksman (E.M.O.M.)

Sir Thomas Lipton
Geoffrey Williams (Peter Davies)

Seule Vingt-cinq Jours Contre l'Atlantique
Edith Baumann (Flammarion)

Rêve de Victoire
Joan de Kat (Arthaud)

Project Cheers
Follett, Newick and Morris (Adlard Coles)

Sailing Alone Around The World
Joshua Slocum (Dover)

Multihull Seamanship
Mike McMullen (Nautical Publishing Co Ltd)

A History of Seamanship
Douglas Phillips Birt (Allen and Unwin)

The Story of American Yachting
William Taylor and Stanley Rosenfield (Appleton Century Grafts)

Solo to America
Frank Page (Adlard Coles)

La Voile Sauvage
Marc Linski (Arthaud)

Lonely Victor
Eric Tabarly (Souvenir Press)

Pen Duick
Eric Tabarly (Adlard Coles)

The Lonely Sea and The Sky
Sir Francis Chichester (Hodder and Stoughton)

Le Tiercé de la Mer
Aymon—Pernet—Chapuis (Solar)

Lonely Voyagers
Jean Merrien (translated by J H Walkins) (Hutchinson)

Come Hell Or High Water
Clare Francis (Pelham)

Index

Page numbers given in *italics* indicate illustrations.

210

212